LITTLE GIRL FOUND

How I Reclaimed My Self
After Early Childhood Trauma

Your support and encouragement in the birthing of this book cannot be measured. — with deep gratitude for your friendship and your being, love, Dawn

Advance Praise for *Little Girl Found*

"In Buddhism, we often speak of 'out of the mud grows the lotus flower.' Author Dawn Nelson's intensely personal and intimate account of the early part of her life could not have been anything but 'mud.' I was happy to learn by the book's end that Dawn had come to realize reconciliation through gratitude, forgiveness, and compassion/love, emerging as a brilliant lotus blossom."

~ Kenneth Kenshin Tanaka, author
Jewels: An Introduction to American Buddhism for Youth... and other books
Professor Emeritus, Musashino University; Shin Buddhist priest

"In *Little Girl Found*, Nelson doesn't tiptoe around any of the painful childhood memories or uncomfortable truths she includes in this heartfelt and ultimately redemptive memoir. She fearlessly reveals her past vulnerabilities and her longing for caring attention as she recounts the darkest moments of her early life. As readers, we follow her successful quest as an adult to find acknowledgement, acceptance, light, and a place of forgiveness."

~ Risa Nye, author
There was a Fire Here: A Memoir

"This riveting book is must-read for all survivors of childhood trauma as well as for the parents, therapists, and educators who work with them. As the author fearlessly delves into the details of her early abandonment, we can recognize moments in our own lives in the narrative. From Dawn Nelson's courageous journey, we learn that earned hope, forgiveness, and gratitude can clear a path to true recovery."

~ Stephan Betz, PhD, MT-BC; CCAP
author, teacher, consultant

"This gift of a book captured me fully and touched me deeply. I ached and cried for that little girl and celebrated the brief moments of blessings, hope and rebellion, then bowed to the Sacred as it expressed itself in the path that Dawn walked and in the transformation she enacted when from the seeds of suffering in her, the ability to heal and bless sprouted and flourished."

~ Joseph Rubano, author, *Go to the Edges*,
Faculty, Center for Biography and Social Art;
counselor; wilderness guide

"Dawn Nelson's newest book invites the reader on an intimate journey as she dives into the psychological and emotional waters of childhood trauma. Her courage in sharing her fierce and tender inquiry into the painful experiences of her early years, illustrates the human heart's capacity to transmute darkness into love and power and demonstrates a timeless truth that is buried at the core of our psychological wounds."

~ Kristina Hunter, Healing Guide;
co-author *Consciousness Medicine*

"This incredibly personal and brave new book has much to give as it reveals how to heal pre-verbal as well as early childhood wounding as the author takes apart her previous narratives and adaptations in an excruciating, bone by bone process."

~ Kathryn Ridall PhD, psychotherapist;
author *Dreaming at the Gates* and other books

"Dawn Nelson's newest book is a uniquely personal, compelling and empowering portrayal of the long-lasting effects of abusive trauma in her infancy and childhood as she takes the reader with her through a transformative, and ultimately, healing journey."

~ Michael Reed Gach, *Acupressure's Potent Points* and other books; acupressure.com Online Healing Programs

"Dawn Nelson has written one of the very best books in the genre of self-revelatory and inspirational spiritual memoirs . . . nuanced, historically broad, a life that truly inspires and a book beautifully written."

~ Stuart Sovatsky PhD, author *Advanced Spiritual Intimacy* and other books; Emeritus Co-president Association for Transpersonal Psychology

"A powerful account of neglect and abandonment, and a courageous healing journey, this beautifully and bravely written book will give anyone wishing to face their own childhood trauma a roadmap and a beacon of hope for a meaningful and fulfilling future."

~ Annelise Hagen, author, *The Yoga Face*

LITTLE GIRL FOUND

How I Reclaimed My Self After Early Childhood Trauma

Dawn Nelson

Foreword by Lawrence Noyes

solificatio
San Francisco, California

Little Girl Found:
How I Reclaimed My Self After Early Childhood Trauma
Copyright © 2021 by Dawn Nelson

No part of this book may be reproduced in any medium without written permission except for short extracts for short quotations embodied in articles or reviews.

First Published by Solificatio
San Francisco, California
2021

ISBN: 978-0-9977619-7-9

Images of the USS Houston in 1938 and of President Roosevelt in his cabin aboard the USS Houston are from the wikimedia.org free media repository.

Photos in Chapter Nine: Brock Palmer; Barry Barankin
Author bio photo: Barry Barankin

Cover and interior book design by Matthew Felix
(https://www.matthewfelix.com)

for

myself, my ancestors, and my descendants

all survivors of life-shaping trauma

and for all who yearn for reconciliation

Contents

Foreword xiii
Preface xv

1. Inception 1
2. Back Story 3
3. Illusions Shattered 8
4. The New (Almost) Mother and Then Another 19
5. The "Home" 31
6. A Few (Nearly) Normal Years 50
7. The Phone Call, the Meeting, and a Visitation 69
8. Ramifications and Reverberations 78
9. Portals to Awakening 91
    Who Am I? 91
    Lessons from the Elderly, the Ill, and the Dying 99
10. Forgiving Esther 107
11. Goddess Descending: The Larger Story 115
12. Stepping Stones on the Path 120
    Gratitude 120
    Blessing 124
    Forgiveness 127

With Gratitude to 132
Suggested Reading 135
About the Author 137

Foreword

When Dawn told me a few years ago that she was writing another book, about traumatic events in her early life and how they affected her, I presumed it was for her family. It's turned out to be so much more.

Dawn takes us on a journey into the nooks and crannies of her unusual life history to make sense of her repeated abandonment and long quest to make the best of it. Orphaned though not really, disconnected from her family yet still somehow connected, she had to contend with these confusing opposites intruding into her life at every turn. In her search for the meaning, she stays devoted and true. This makes her story something for all of us. It's simply time well spent to see and feel what happens when a young girl's heart always stays just a little larger than the life circumstances that could collapse it.

It was nearly forty years ago, in the time covered in Chapter Nine, that I met Dawn. This was when the deeper parts of her inner search began to flower. She was curious about who she really is and ready to dive into its mysteries using any method that held promise. As I got to know her, I noticed that her characteristic default position in life was good humor and well-wishes for everybody. The value of this approach always struck me as the best one possible, and it was easy to build a friendship on it. In time, I came to know Dawn as one of those special people you may reliably visit and leave feeling good about the person and good about yourself as well.

By now, I know that we won't look deeper into anything unless we have good reason to do so, which seems to be a hidden function of life's pain if we choose to select that option. Dawn's journey led her to more than just a healing for herself. It awakened in her a life purpose of ministering, through the therapeutic model of skilled and compassionate touch she created, to the elderly, the ill, and the dying. It led to something great coming through her and breaking new ground in the field of caregiving. This unsought consequence of her search emerges from her narrative unexpectedly and, for me, validates her efforts even more.

This book is about a lonely young girl making her way from abandonment and trauma and emerging a grace-bestowing goddess. It's about the search for who we really are and the most profound kinship we have that serves as a North Star if we let it, despite whatever life throws our way. Dawn's journey, which is in many ways our journey, is a compelling and inspirational read.

Lawrence Noyes, author
The Enlightenment Intensive: The Power of Dyad Communication for Self-Realization
Fernandina Beach, Florida

Preface

We are healed when we can grow from our suffering, when we can reframe it as an act of grace that leads us back to who we truly are.
— Joan Borysenko

It is how we respond to trauma that determines whether it will turn us into stone or whether it will be a spiritual teacher.
— Peter A. Levine

One balmy May evening, sitting in a lush and sweet-smelling garden with a few friends, I heard my youngest adult daughter speaking about my first few years of life. As my husband cut in a couple times to correct or expand on some detail or other, I noted that my loved ones' retelling of a story shared with them in bits and pieces through the years, and filtered through their perceptions, differed somewhat from what I considered "my story."

The script in my head, about a barely one-year-old child left alone in her crib for three days and nights, finally rescued by police after calls from concerned neighbors, was spawned from a few primary source materials and my paternal grandmother's memories. Each retelling, along with my changing thoughts and beliefs as decades passed, added weight to the storyline.

If we repeat a tale often enough, whether to ourselves or to others, it gains traction, affecting the way we think and feel about ourselves. We believe the story. We identify who we are with the story. It influences our behaviors and colors the choices we make in life. Yet at some point we begin to understand that whatever may have taken place, it is our thoughts about those events that keep replaying the movie in our heads.

Writing has long provided solace and sustenance in my life. My locked childhood diaries served as confidants. Drafting fictional stories helped assuage my loneliness as a child, and fueled my adolescent daydreams. Years of journaling taught me that the act of putting pen, or pencil, to paper about anything in our lives can often clarify thoughts and spark shifts in awareness.

My books, *Compassionate Touch: Hands on Caregiving for the Elderly, the Ill and the Dying* and, a few years later, *From the Heart Through the Hands: The Power of Touch in Caregiving* helped elucidate what I had learned in working with those in later life stages, and provided further support for participants in my training workshops. The healing power of writing became abundantly clear to me during my ovarian cancer diagnosis, treatment, and recovery in my mid-fifties. What began as a record of the dialogue I was having with my body in the chemotherapy infusion room led to the publishing of *Making Friends with Cancer*.

Mental health researchers tell us that the act of writing itself helps integrate different parts of the brain in healing from the often long-lasting effects of trauma. Social psychologist James Pennebaker observed that incorporating our thoughts and emotions while writing about trauma not only brings new understanding in regard to such events, but can help us resolve them. *Little Girl Found: How I Reclaimed My Self After Early Childhood Trauma*, emerged from a belief that acknowledgement and acceptance are the first steps in relinquishing one's "story," and that purposeful investigation of any life-shaping trauma can lead to mental and emotional release of that which is still taking up space in one's body, brain, and heart. I chose to look backwards in order to move forward in a less encumbered and more authentic way.

As often happens, once we commit to a task, support arrives in unexpected ways. With a bit of patient and persistent sleuthing, I was able to obtain legal documents from the state of Kentucky which I had never known existed. Originally thinking I might be able to locate a police report or records from the hospital where I was taken the night I was rescued from my crib, I was ill prepared emotionally to read the thick envelope of legal papers that eventually arrived, revealing difficult to assimilate details in regard to my birth mother's chronic neglect and rejection.

Reading and transcribing dozens of letters exchanged between my father and his third wife written over a number of months in 1948, which I'd had in my possession for a decade yet never read, added to the emotional turmoil of my undertaking, as did studying recorded interviews conducted with my father during the last year of his life. Those conversations had begun with a casual question I asked my father while sitting with him in the waiting area of a Veterans Administration hospital in northern California before he was admitted to begin an experimental cancer chemotherapy protocol. Our dialogue ended close to a year later at my father's bedside in his home in Arkansas shortly before his death. Nuances that had gone unnoticed during that distressing year flashed out at me like beacons thirty years later.

Writing *Little Girl Found* supported me in uncovering and exploring a wounding that I had never fully or consciously accepted. My writing process intensified as memories took on new meaning, from my current perspective, awakening energy that had been stuck in my physical body for most of my life, and became increasingly therapeutic while uncovering ways in which my early trauma had influenced my adult behaviors. The pursuit became more and more healing as I listened to, embraced and reconciled with the wounded child inside me.

An endeavor more demanding and intense than I could have imagined, writing *Little Girl Found* helped illuminate my path on a journey through recognizing, acknowledging, accepting, embracing, reframing, forgiving and—ultimately—liberating myself from a narrative which had, in subtle ways, continued to hold my psyche hostage for decades.

We are all shaped by the circumstances of our lives. However, as Holocaust survivor Viktor Frankl famously wrote, and a number of spiritual teachers have reiterated, we have the power to choose how we respond to whatever may occur. We can let our wounds cripple us or we can allow them to inform and transform us. I believe we all have a responsibility to let our voices be heard, to share our stories in order to help each other heal. Facing the darkness in our lives is how we rediscover the infinite force of our light. It is my hope that my journey may in some way support you on your own, whether you are a survivor, a seeker, a helper, or a healer.

MOTHER PLACED UNDER SUSPENDED JAIL SENTENCE headlines the article on the front page of the KENTUCKY TIMES-STAR for Thursday, September 14, 1944. The news story states that the 24-year-old mother was given a jail sentence of 30 days when she pleaded guilty to a charge of neglecting her 13-month-old daughter. The county juvenile officer is quoted as saying she had received numerous complaints about the alleged failure of the mother in caring for the child, leaving the child alone in the home, going out and coming back at a late hour . . . The judge ordered the child placed in the custody of her paternal grandparents pending a further order from the court and severely reprimanded the young mother. The article ends by stating that "the child has been in Speers Hospital since early last Sunday, and that the father has not seen his daughter."

    That child was me . . .

—Author

Chapter One

Inception

Write what disturbs you, what you fear, what you have not been willing to speak about. Be willing to be split open. . . When you heal yourself, you're helping everyone.
—Natalie Goldberg

My three children were flourishing as adults; and I was enjoying several grandchildren before I was led to revisit a narrative I had long held in regard to my first few years of life. Extensive biological and developmental research has now shown that consequential neglect—the ongoing disruption or significant absence of caregiver responsiveness—can cause more harm to a young child's development than overt physical abuse. Neuroscientists have learned that the most crucial stage for brain development is the first year of life. They are even able to articulate distinct ways in which specific kinds of early childhood abuse impact the developing brain.

I truly thought I had dealt with my "abandonment issues" during countless hours of cognitive and somatic therapy sessions, and various meditative practices. As new evidence of my biological mother's persistent neglect in my first year of life was revealed, and I began recognizing and remembering subsequent abandonments, I thought I might drown in the sea of sadness that began to engulf me. I wondered if I could survive experiencing the long-denied pain of the wounding, much less the anger smoldering beneath.

Perhaps poet Emily Dickinson was right when she wrote:

> There is a pain — so utter —
> It covers substance up —

Perhaps there are psychic woundings so completely unrecognizable and untenable to an infant that the being is swallowed up. She disappears inside the agony—of not being seen, of not being heard, of not being valued—creating a profound voice in her subconscious. With nobody to mirror the reality, the small being forgets who she actually is. She shapes a mask from whatever models are nearby, and then begins to create a persona to go with it. She structures a story, a belief system, such as, "I'm not good enough" or "I don't deserve to be loved."

> Then covers the Abyss with Trance —
> So memory can step
> Around — across — upon it

The child falls asleep to her true nature and forgets that which the mind cannot yet comprehend, in order to survive.

> As one within a Swoon —
> Goes safely — where an open eye —
> Would drop Him — Bone by Bone.

Wrapped in the cocoon of forgetfulness, the growing child can feel safe and protected. She can forgo fully experiencing the pain of separation and rejection, thus averting a slow and agonizing fall into a chasm of darkness. Eventually, however, the longing for Self prevails. There comes a time when it is no longer possible to avoid the Abyss, when there is nowhere else to go, when there is nothing else to do but to face the demons who lurk in the darkness that blocks out the light of knowing.

Chapter Two
Back Story

We all are the continuation of our fathers, our mothers, our ancestors...
—Thich Nhat Hanh

A mother is a child's first looking glass into the world.
—Rachelle E. Goodrich

In 1941, the man who would become my father was twenty-two years old. A precocious musician from a young age, having played professionally when he was still in high school, he quit college after one year to continue his musical career. In 1936, he was playing in a Cincinnati, Ohio ballroom and getting other jobs through the musicians' union when his father heard about a new naval program in Washington, D.C. for musicians. Many years later, during an interview with my father that had begun with a casual question I had asked about his musical history, he recounted what happened next.

> Ken:
> So, I went to D.C. to try out for the program. There was a big deal made of this in the local papers and all about my appointment, and my picture was in the paper and everything. And it gave me a swelled head, to the extent that when they announced I'd made it, I couldn't very well say I didn't want it.
>
> Dawn:
> You didn't really want to go? Why not?
>
> Ken:
> It was the adulation that made me go. And the training was virtu-

ally nothing. They simply didn't give you what they said in writing they would. It was supposed to be similar to going to Juilliard or the Cincinnati School of Music or some comparable place where you would get intensive musical training. But that wasn't what it turned out to be. It was more like basic training with a service organization, including training on how to survive as a navy man. There was almost no musical training at all and that wasn't what I'd signed up for.

As it turned out, fate intervened for my father and he was able to escape the situation he had unhappily found himself in.

Ken:
There were some people there who knew of my dislike of the whole set up and these guys were due to graduate. They had a band formed and just needed a good clarinet and sax man to get assigned to their unit so they went to the guy in charge of bands and told him their situation and he made an exception.

The band played at the 1939 World's Fair in New York City for six months before boarding the USS Phoenix for that ship's "shakedown cruise," which covered the entire east coast of South America and the Panama Canal before returning to the Florida coast, and disembarking in South Carolina. The musicians were then transferred to the USS Houston (a heavy cruiser commissioned in 1930 and sunk in 1942), the ship said to be FDR's favorite when he was surveying the fleet, presiding over mock battles, or sometimes just going deep sea fishing. In a daily record my father kept during his time on this ship, he mentions  President Roosevelt engaging in two of those activities, writing about the band assembling on the deck FDR in his cabin on USS Houston to play honors each time the president returned to the ship after his fishing excursions and commenting on the great effort it took him to move his legs.

After being discharged from the navy, my father was looking for work in Los Angeles, in order to get his musician's union card, when he received a letter advising him to report for induction into the armed services. Unlike other young men of his time, or so we are given to believe, my father admitted towards the end of his life that he hadn't actually considered being in the military an especially honorable obligation or heroic pursuit. He did add that he was really "anti-regiment" as well as "pretty cocky" at that time of his life.

FDR in his cabin on the USS Houston

> Ken:
> I was convinced that I would go in there and tell them I'd been in the navy and they'd say, 'We can't use you!' But they said 'Health—A-OK.' I argued with the sergeant and even went to the chaplain, but the next day I was on the troop train going to Ft. Benning, Georgia.

According to my father, he met the woman who would give birth to me at Daytona Beach, Florida, while on a weekend pass. "Just like all the other soldiers, out for a good time." Presumably, she was one among many young women also looking for some fun with a soldier. A twenty-one-year-old divorcée, she called herself Penny. It is unclear exactly how many days or hours Penny and my father actually spent in each other's physical company prior to their marriage, which took place in Ft. Thomas, Kentucky shortly before Christmas. The faded newspaper clipping announcing the marriage says the groom was on a fifteen-day furlough, also revealing that the

bride wore "a wool frock . . . and a gardenia corsage." The last line of the announcement mentions that "the couple will pass the next week at the home of the groom's parents before moving into their apartment in Baker Village at Ft. Benning."

Nearly fifty years later, during an afternoon of recorded reminiscing with his two sisters, my father recalls being "shipped out" with the 2nd Armored Division of the US Army, about a year after his marriage, in December of 1942. His younger sister, Bobbie, then asked a question about where Penny went when he shipped overseas, generating the following dialogue.

> Ken:
> Oh, she went back to her mother in Daytona. Then when she found out that she was pregnant, she came to Ft. Thomas to stay with the folks.
>
> Bobbie:
> Was that her idea?
>
> Ken:
> I think it was Mom's . . . I'm not sure.
>
> Bobbie:
> You'd think she'd want to be with her own mother.
>
> Ken:
> Oh, not <u>her</u> mother! That was Penny's <u>problem</u>, her mother!

This rather vehement declaration by my father in regard to his first mother-in-law is not elaborated on, although there were other hints here and there that would lead one to believe she was a fairly narcissistic and manipulative woman, as well as a heavy drinker. It is likely that she was an alcoholic, as her only daughter would become, given that both genes and environment are known to play a role in that addiction.

In a recorded conversation with my father about six months before his death, I asked him if he knew Penny was pregnant before he left to go overseas.

Ken:
No. She told me in a letter.

Dawn:
How did you feel when you got that news?

Ken:
I was very, very pleased.

    I failed to ask my father if his then wife had shared any thoughts regarding how she felt about being pregnant or about the prospect of giving birth, nor did I ask if she had been trying to get pregnant before he went overseas. He didn't recall being consulted about names, saying he was "taken aback" when he was told she chose the name Dawn because it was so unusual.

    Information beyond my birth certificate concerning my actual entrance into this world is scarce. My father remembered Penny saying in a letter, "There is no way I'm going to give birth without drugs." She moved out of my grandparents' house shortly after my birth into her own apartment. It is fairly obvious in statements Penny makes about my grandmother in her letters to my father during the following year that she valued her own independence and ideas more than any help or advice offered from the mother of her husband, who had raised three children.

    My father's draft into the Army was for one year though, as he stated:

> . . . but then the war came two months before my option was up and until the war was over, there <u>was</u> no option. I asked for an emergency leave when you were born, and it finally came through almost two years later.

    I was eighteen months old the first time I saw my father in person for a short time before he returned to the service. At that time, my mother having been declared unfit to care for me, I had been in my grandparents' custody for five months.

Chapter Three

Illusions Shattered

In order to grow from an experience, we first of all have to acknowledge an experience. This is particularly true in the case of trauma.
—Steve Taylor

When the large envelope from the Kentucky Department for Libraries and Archives arrives, it is thicker than I expected. I hesitate before opening it, surprised by the trickle of trepidation I'm feeling, along with my eagerness to search the contents. Inside the envelope I find twenty-five pages of copied legal documents, along with the divorce decree releasing my father from the bonds of matrimony with Grace Elise Armor (the woman known as Penny) date stamped April 25, 1945. There are three legal depositions: one with my father, Kenneth C. Armor, one with my grandfather, Claude A. Amor and one with Laurel Lyons, probation officer. At the time the depositions were taken, my father had been in the US Army over four years, overseas for two and a half of those.

The longest deposition is with my father and I read it first. After a few identifying, preliminary questions, the examining lawyer asks if he heard from his wife regularly while he was overseas, and my father answers: "Not after the first year." Attorney Scott then directs him to read a salient paragraph or two from a letter he received from his wife, dated June 21, 1944.

> I didn't think I would ever come to the point of asking you what I am about to while you were overseas, thinking it would be kinder to wait until you returned. However, you seem to be doing a lot of planning for the future and frankly I don't feel that we have one together. I have met someone with whom I am very much in love

and want nothing more than to spend the rest of my life with him. I would be willing to do the right thing about the baby, that is let you see or have her as often as the Court ordained.

Was she drunk? Delusional? Was she simply using me as a pawn to manipulate my father? Did she think of me as just a possession?

Although it was not referred to in the court proceedings that day, I have another handwritten letter from Penny to my father, dated less than two weeks later, July 9, 1944. In a long, rambling message in which, among a number of other complaints, she tells my father to "tell your mother she does not have to feel responsible for my welfare in any way any longer. I would rather be left alone." She then says that she thinks her last letter to him was written because she was feeling lonely and vulnerable, followed by the sentence: "If we get back together, I think I could love you almost as much as I once did, but I would prefer that you make the decision," before adding:

> There is one job I have been working at for the last eleven months that your mother or anyone else cannot say I have failed at and that is the raising of my child. I feel if we should separate, I am entitled to the baby since I have done it all by myself. I'm sure you will agree.

Perusing these words again, more than 60 years after they were penned, juxtaposed with the depositions I have in front of me now, is unnerving. It awakens both shock and compassion in me, along with multiple questions.

Did she actually believe what was she saying? Is this what is meant by alcoholic brain? Was it a cunning attempt to control or punish my father? How irrational was she? Was she suffering from a mental disorder or perhaps a bad case of postpartum depression? Or was it simply classic narcissism?

The attorney continues questioning my father.

> Q: You know now, since your return, that your wife apparently has no interest in the child, is that correct?

A: Yes, only a selfish interest, that is to want to possess her without sharing any responsibility.

No interest in the child! Can that really be true? Did she ever feel any emotional attachment to me at all? I am hit by a wave of anger, grief, and sadness—for me, for my father and for the woman who brought me into the world yet who was apparently unable to accept or see me as anything but an inconvenience. My mouth stretches wide as a protracted, piercing AAAAAAAAAHHHHHHHH bursts forth before hissing and growling sounds emerge. I feel my face morph into some kind of cat-like creature with teeth bared defensively. My hands rise upwards to the sides of my face, my fingers curling . . .

The next part of my father's deposition concerns the amount of money Penny was receiving monthly at that time: $150.00 from her guardian—income from a trust fund left to her by her biological father—in addition to a governmental allotment of $80 per month once I was born. My father adds that before my birth, "She received on average of $130.00 a month" from him. A quick bit of research tells me that the total sum of money she had at her disposal after my arrival was more than the average wage for all occupations in 1943.

If Penny didn't want to call on my grandparents for babysitting relief, why wouldn't she have hired help, when she clearly had enough money to do so? Why wouldn't she have offered to pay a neighbor in her apartment building to look after me when she wanted to go out or have a little time to herself? What kept her from asking a neighbor to at least check on me occasionally, if she left me sleeping when she went out?

As the questioning continues, my father reports that upon his arrival in Ft. Thomas on the leave he was finally granted, he spent a few days with me and his parents before he then took me "to the residence his wife had established for herself, in order to try and work things out with her."

Q: Why did you take the child back to your parents' home?

A: Because my wife would not take care of the child, and also because she requested that I do that.

> Q: What is her attitude toward this child of hers and yours?
>
> A: She is quite frank about it. She says she does not want the child to interfere with her own personal life.

My father goes on to describe the specific event that persuaded him that "this was not going to work."

> My wife had asked me if I wanted to stay in a picture show this particular evening, and she would take care of the child, she would take her home. When I came out of the show, I found her in the corner cafe drinking beer, and she was with two soldiers. I asked her if she would like to go to the show and I would take care of the baby. She said she would. That night she came in about 12:30 a.m. rather drunk which of course meant that the next morning, she had to get over the night before.

My emotions are roiling. I feel as if I am flotsam riding the waves of a raging sea crashing against a rocky shore. Exhausted and unsettled by the words I am reading, yet engrossed, I press on in pursuit of details surrounding this critical part of my infancy. Recognizing the name Laurel Lyons as the Probation Officer quoted in the now yellowed newspaper clipping about my birth mother's arrest, I turn to her deposition. Once her history, seven and a half years as Probation Officer for Campbell County, and connection with the case are established, Ms. Lyons is asked to "recite what you know of Mrs. Armor's attitude and conduct toward her child." Ms. Lyon speaks of receiving a number of complaints from neighbors in the building and in the neighborhood about a Mrs. Penny Armor "neglecting the baby, leaving the baby alone day and night whenever she went out."

> Many times, when Mrs. Armor would be out in the afternoon, different friends would ask her where the baby was, and many times the baby was home where there was never anyone to attend to it . . . Another lady that lived in the building said that if Mrs. Armor took a notion to go out, if only she would just have left the door open, so that they could have gotten to the baby if anything had happened. Another neighbor had said that Penny would be out all night many nights. The next day it was necessary to sleep

all day and the baby was just in the house without any attention.

And just like that I am yanked out of my illusions. I can no longer protect myself by even pretending to believe the story I often hoped might be true: my birth mother was inexperienced, depressed, tired, and terribly lonely. She left me alone after I went to sleep at night a few times to have a drink at a nearby bar. One night she had too much to drink, met someone who took advantage of her loneliness, someone who had no idea she'd left a sleeping baby alone in an apartment. He took her to his place to sleep it off and she was so exhausted she didn't wake up for a night and a day, or maybe she woke in such a confused state that she somehow just let herself momentarily forget about her baby.

I must accept the fact that the woman whose physical body afforded me passage into this world wasn't just unprepared for or overwhelmed by motherhood, she was actually unwilling, or unable, to embrace that role, to bond with me or to put caring for me above her own desires and addictions. Her neglect was chronic and ongoing. I was an inconvenience. I wasn't valued. I wasn't embraced. I wasn't claimed. I was left unattended repeatedly, uncared for and, essentially, unmothered during the first year of my life.

Ms. Lyons goes on to testify about the night she "had to take the baby," recounting how, after receiving a telephone call around 10:00 p.m. regarding the baby crying in a darkened apartment, she moved immediately to get a warrant, then "got two Ft. Thomas police who proceeded to go the home of Mrs. Armor with me."

If there were numerous complaints, why wasn't some action not taken sooner? What was it that compelled Ms. Lyons to act so quickly on that particular autumn evening? What was different that time? Had the same person called previously? And what caused her, or him, to call that particular night at that hour? Anger? Frustration? Compassion?

My mind jumps back to the summer of my twelfth birthday when my beloved grandparents were visiting. My grandmother and my father asked me to sit down with them on the sofa facing the big picture window in the new three-bedroom brick house where my father, my stepmother, Ruth Ann, and I were living.

> Daddy is perched on the arm of the couch. I am sitting between him and Nana who is saying that she thinks I am old enough to know what they are about to tell me. Nana glances at my father before saying, 'When you were just over one year old, your mother left you alone for three days and nights. The police came and they found you and you were taken to the hospital for a few days, and after that you came to live with us.' She smiles and squeezes my hand. I smile back and return her squeeze.

The deeper significance of my grandmother's words fell on deaf ears, one might say—at the time—either because my mind was preoccupied with preteen fantasies or, possibly, because I wasn't ready to cope with such a revelation. I don't think I asked any questions. After Nana said her piece, my father handed me a large envelope with a file folder inside, telling me I should save the information, keep the documents safe and look through them whenever I was ready to do so. It would be a couple years before I gave them more than a cursory read-through and a couple decades before I would peruse them in any depth before setting them aside again.

As I return to Ms. Lyon's testimony, I read: "We were unable to rouse anyone upon our arrival at the home. We then entered the apartment through the living room window."

They must have knocked several times on the door perhaps loudly, before deciding to come in through a window which presumably they were able to open without breaking the glass. Had others already knocked on the door? Do I have some pre-verbal sense memory in me from that time that is responsible for my sensitivity to loud noises, especially in the middle of the night when I wake up, startled and anxious, wondering if I've dreamed the door-knocking sounds I hear so distinctly or if it was real?

Ms. Lyons details the disarray that greeted them once they were inside the apartment—dirty dishes on the table and counters, uneaten food in pots and pans on the stove, an empty beer jug, remains of other alcoholic drinks, an unmade bed, a messy bathroom, and so on.

It looked as if there might have been a party there and they just left it that way. We walked into the bedroom where the baby was in bed. She was awake, and there were two other glasses there, each filled with a highball. I proceeded to take the baby out of the bed and look for clothes for her.

More questions vie for my attention. I presume Ms. Lyons needed to find clothing for me because whatever I was wearing, along with the crib mattress and the coverings, was wet and soiled. Why, I wonder, did she mention the two highball glasses near my bed?

Was the door to the bedroom where she found me open or closed? Was I able to hear noises from the street or from the other apartments in the building? Was there a window in the bedroom where she found me? Was there a light left on anywhere in the apartment? Could the condition I was found in have anything to do with my lifelong aversion to being cold, with my chronic constipation long into adulthood, with the fear that followed me throughout my childhood, and much of my adulthood, of being alone in the dark? Is it possible that my lifetime distaste for alcohol in all forms could be traced back to an ever present smell of alcohol in my infancy?

I notice that I am never mentioned by name in the deposition. I am always referred to as "the infant," "the baby," "the child," or even as "it."

Ms. Lyons goes on with her account of the night in question. "I took the baby from there and placed it in Speers Hospital. In other words, the baby would have been alone all that night if I hadn't taken her." She says that she left the warrant with the policemen "who waited until a car pulled up at about 4:30 a.m."

Tears spring to my eyes as a question I've often pondered is answered. I feel a rush of gratitude toward this young woman with the alliterative name now etched in my mind, for her care and compassion that September night so long ago. I experience a wave of immense relief at being discovered, noticed, touched, being rescued from the darkness.

The attorney continues questioning Mr. Lyons.

> Q: What was Penny Armor's plea to the charge in the County Court?

> A: Guilty.

> Q: What did Judge Bertelsman do with respect to the custody of the child?
>
> A: He gave the custody to the grandmother.

And so I learn the name of the judge who, in my grandmother's recounting of this moment when I asked her about it a number of years later stated, "The judge said to your mother, 'Do you understand that you are relinquishing all rights to this child from this day forward?'" My grandmother said "Penny replied, 'yes' and the judge then instructed her to hand you to me."

Was I awake or asleep in that moment? Did I have a bottle, a toy or blanket that I was holding onto as the transfer was made? What was the woman who had given birth to me experiencing in that instant? Did she hesitate, shed any tears? Did she feel any distress, or remorse? Or was she just relieved to relinquish the responsibilities she'd had such a difficult time accepting? What was I sensing or experiencing as the transfer was made?

Toward the end of Ms. Lyon's deposition, I learn that part of the court's order that day was that Penny would be allowed to visit me at my grandparent's home if she so chose, "though she did not make her visits very often," Ms. Lyons added.

> Q: You continued your investigation to find out what her attitude was toward the child?
>
> A: Yes. I just could not see that there was any motherly love there at all for the baby. . .that is abnormal.

I gasp for breath as I cradle myself with my arms. I begin speaking to that small child that lives inside me, "You are okay now, you're alive. We survived, we are safe, we are loved." My body rocks forwards and backwards. A tsunami of tears cascades like a waterfall over my face, dripping off my chin and wetting my clothing as I give myself permission, at long last, to acknowledge the despair, to mourn for that part of me that was left alone, crying, hungry, confused. My teeth begin to chatter. I am shivering. I manage to leave my computer chair and stumble to the nearest bed where I turn onto my side and curl up into a fetal position. Unfamiliar, high-pitched sounds I cannot stop are coming out of my throat. My eyes are closed. I am gulping air. Eventually, my sobs begin to subside and my tear-stained skin dries, salty on my face. I am no longer shivering. I open my eyes to sunlight blanketing the bed and welcome its warmth. My breathing normalizes. I listen to the silence as I gaze out the window at wispy white clouds moving slowly across a beautiful azure sky. A red-tailed hawk with an enormous wing span soars through the air, then tips its wings, and swoops below the clouds disappearing from sight. I breathe deeply. I return to my adult body.

Sitting at my desk a few hours later, I finish reading Ms. Lyon's deposition. When she is questioned about her follow-up visits to the home of the child's grandparents and what kind of home it was, Ms. Lyons answers: "It is just lovely, a real home." Asked if the child was receiving the proper attention while she was there, she responds, "It certainly was." The probation officer's deposition ends with a final question from the attorney.

> Q: You feel like the custody of that child should remain with its grandparents?
>
> A: Yes I do.

. . . . .

The shortest deposition is with my father's father, whom I called Granny. His answers to the questions asked of him are straightforward, succinct and without embellishment, just as I remember he himself being. I experience a rush of gratitude for my grandfather thinking about his quiet, gentle strength and how protected I felt in his arms, based on memories of him from my very early childhood and from photographs my grandmother saved and passed on to me.

One unphotographed experience involving him remains embedded in my memory.

> Nana buys me a big red balloon that floats in the air. I am carrying it proudly, tied around my right wrist as we walk to the house. I am excited to show this wonderful new thing to Granny. Nana is behind me, holding onto my left hand, helping me as I slowly navigate the wooden steps into the basement where Granny is at his workbench against the right wall. The balloon bursts suddenly! I break into tears, scared by the unexpected loud noise and brokenhearted by the disappearance of my most wonderful gift. Granny comes quickly to the stairs. He doesn't talk. He just holds me until I stop crying.

My grandfather's testimony includes the fact that Penny lived just "a little over a mile away, a short streetcar ride to within two blocks" of their home. He states that her court-sanctioned visits to me, after they took me to their home, occurred every couple of weeks in the beginning "but became less and less frequent, usually lasting only a half hour or less."

When he was questioned about his daughter-in-law's attitude toward the child my grandfather responds: "She showed no particular interest during her visits." This seems to help explain why, in the first photograph of me that exists today of me with Penny at that age, clearly taken at my grandparents' house, I am looking at her as if I don't know who she is, and seem to be a bit wary of her.

My grandfather is asked if there was any "other activity that would indicate Penny did not want to be burdened with the child." He answers that "she had her phone number removed from listings and would not give it to us."

The words of Ms. Lyons, my father, and my grandfather swim and circle in my head like feathers in a breeze:

"no maternal instincts"
"no motherly love at all for the baby"
"complete disregard for any motherly duties"
"unnatural"
"not normal"
"appeared to have no interest in the child"
"doesn't want the child to interfere with her own personal life"

Unexpectedly, I hear my grandmother's answer to a question I had once asked her—after experiencing labor and childbirth myself twice—about what my birth had been like for my mother. "She considered it a long, painful and ultimately disappointing ordeal when she didn't see the boy she was hoping for." I let the words she said sink in and rest in my consciousness now in a way that I didn't when my grandmother uttered them.

Would my mother have behaved differently if I had been a boy? Did all this happen just because I came into this life in a female body?

Struggling to keep my heart and mind open, I surrender to the revelations of the collective depositions. A lump form in my throat and extends downward. My chest tightens as my body shakes with quiet sobs until I take a large gulp of air and, without warning, a seemingly endless, shrill wail emerges from somewhere deep in my psyche. I feel the pain of every child who has ever cried for a mother, a father, or a caregiver who didn't answer, for every child who has ever been left alone, ignored, forgotten, mistreated, rejected, neglected, abandoned. I weep for all the infants and young children who weren't rescued, who weren't taken in by loving relatives as I was for a time. I weep for children everywhere who are at this very moment being exploited, misused, and abused in unimaginable and horrific ways, for the children of all ages who are suffering ongoing, unspeakable trauma. I let my heart break open and bleed.

Chapter Four

The New (Almost) Mother and Then Another

The crucial aspect of abuse is not what occurred but what impact it had on you, how you explained it to yourself...and how it has affected your life.
—Eliana Gil, PhD

Most people think of trauma as what happens to us but trauma is what happens inside us as a result of what happened to us.
—Gabor Maté

During a reorganizing binge shortly after my youngest child is safely settled in college in another state, I come across a collection of oversized negatives in an envelope inside a small box, along with a few black-and-white photos of my father taken during WWII. Examining the negatives closely I see one with three people: a man, a woman and a young child. I think it likely that the man is my father and the child is me. I am curious enough about the woman to track down a place that will digitalize negatives from the 1940s. Peering at the printed photograph, I see my father looking ever so slightly smug, with me sitting on his shoulders, a thin-lipped, half smile on my face. My father and I are both looking at the person taking the picture, most likely my grand-

mother. The woman in the photograph, I suddenly realize, is the seldom mentioned Ginger.

My father's new bride is looking up at me, a bit dubiously it seems. Perhaps she is wondering what she has gotten herself into with this quick marriage that comes with a little girl, not yet two years old, whom she is just now meeting for the first time? As I study Ginger's face and demeanor, I suddenly burst into tears.

Why didn't you think a little harder before marrying somebody with such a young child before you'd even met her? Did you even want to be a mother? What did I do to drive you away? Was it the bed wetting? The recurrent bronchitis I've been told I already had by that time in my life? How quickly did it dawn on you that you'd made a mistake? Did anyone caution you to think twice before you accepted such a hasty proposal?

I hear myself nearly shout, "We could have been a **family**!" When my husband walks into the room and asks who I am yelling at, I show him the picture of the threesome and explain who Ginger is. He sees something in the image I seem to have missed, remarking, "Nobody in that photo is really claiming you—not your father or this lady he married so hastily." He then points to another photo I've had developed, one of me with my grandmother. "You can feel the love in this photograph. You can see that this person is claiming you. She's watching over you and loving you. This woman is saying, 'I've got your back. I'm here for you no matter what'."

My tears flow even faster. Remembering the unconditional love that I received from my grandmother, I am flooded with emotion, wonderstruck by the depth of gratitude I feel for my grandparents, for the commitment they made by taking me into their home and caring for me at that stage in my life and theirs. I am keenly aware of the profound significance of their love and devotion which interrupted the cycle of toxic stress in my infancy and no doubt saved me from what might have been far more serious consequences in my development going forward.

Searching for what my father says about his second wife in interviews I conducted with him in 1989, I locate the section where he talks about his release from the Army. He had been sent to Ft. Ord, on the Central California coast, until the war was over and, after that, to Camp Beale Air Force Base for discharge. The Army then paid for his flight to Los Angeles since that's where he'd been living when inducted. He was looking for work in LA when he received a wire from his roommate from the Army, drummer Tom Dribble.

> He wanted to know if I'd want a job with Lloyd LaBrie who was going on the road to see if he could make it. . . I was tickled to death to hear from somebody that I knew and to get work, so I said yes. The band was on the way to Kansas City so I joined them there . . . I met Ginger in Kansas City and then the band was playing in Youngstown, Ohio and I called her up and said, "How'd you like to get married?" She said OK and she flew up to Youngstown and we got married.

Whoa! What? Who does such a thing? What were you thinking? What was she thinking? When did you tell her you had a child? Did you show her a picture of me and she said I was cute? How old was she? Did either of you have a clue about what being a parent actually requires?

Thirty years have passed since I transcribed my father's words. When I heard them, all I said to him was: "Kind of a short courtship! And then what?"

> Ken:
> I left the band then and went to Cincinnati. . .we stayed with the folks and I got jobs easily. After about three months, Ginger decided she wasn't a mother and took off to Kansas City on the pretext of visiting an aunt, or sister, but really, she was leaving me. She later wrote and asked for money to get a divorce. It was really kind of devious because she had already gotten the divorce. I wrote to the Kansas Courts to see if she'd filed for divorce. They wrote back and said, yes she was divorced.

Dawn:
You could get divorced without you even knowing it or signing a paper or anything?

Ken:
Oh, they would just say she was abandoned. I wasn't around so it was abandonment and why look any further into the matter?

Dawn:
Were you upset? Did you really love her?

Ken:
I suppose I loved her at the time but it wasn't a deep love. To be honest it was a marriage to get you a mother . . .

What on earth made you think that a woman you barely knew would want a child, let alone that she would instantly become a devoted mother to one she'd never met? What evidence did you have that made you believe that? Did you just think any woman would jump at the chance to be a mother if she could also be the wife of a good-looking professional musician? Was it your arrogance? Ignorance? Lust?

Summarizing that period of time in our lives, my father said:

> I had gotten married and hoped that my new wife would become your devoted mother which didn't work out that way at all, as you know. Anyway, I played the season, in the pit band at the Albee for live shows. They had a different show in every week that ran seven days a week, early matinee and then evening.

By April or May of 1946, before I had turned three, my father was living in San Diego, California where he had taken a job playing in a band at a nightclub called Sherman's. I remained with my grandparents, who were providing me with consistent and loving care.

My father wrote the following about the night he met my next stepmother.

> It was a Monday evening, my night off from work. I was playing with Jimmy James Orchestra at the time and Ruth Ann was

The New (Almost) Mother and Then Another

working there. I had contemplated asking her for a date for some time and had finally obtained the courage to ask her. Behold, she accepted. After she finished work, I drove her home—a beach house occupied by five other girls. We spent the evening talking & talking & talking and even went in swimming. The rest is history.

Ruth Ann, who was then 25, and working at Sherman's Nightclub as a cigarette girl, wrote:

> The first night I ever noticed Kenneth was May 27, 1946. Since he was off work, he proceeded to come in and bother me as I was doing mine. I finally made a date with him for after work. We rode around first and then went to my house. We talked lots, played records and went swimming. Much to my surprise I had a wonderful time. We started going quite steady and soon cared very much for each other.

According to Ruth Ann's written record of that time, she and my father left San Diego in the fall, stopping to see her family in Kansas and watching a World Series game in St. Louis "before we headed to Nana & Granny's house."

> We lived there with them until we came back to Wichita and got married. You were still wetting the bed at three years old—emotional stress. I had a room across from yours and every night you dropped your socks out of the crib. You didn't call me mommy, just Ruthie, and I didn't push myself on you.

Why would I call her mommy? Did my father introduce her to me as my new mommy? Is that what I was told about Ginger? Was Ruth told by someone that I was wetting the bed because of emotional stress or was that something she just decided for herself? I remember Nana talking about me throwing my socks out of the crib and then crying or calling her and she would come give them back to me. Did I fling my socks to the floor to see if somebody would come give them back to me, to prove to myself that I wasn't all alone Why was it so important to me to keep my socks in bed with me at night?

Ruth describes the schedule in the expanded household during those months.

> I was working for Lever Brothers and went to work every morning with Granny who worked for Westinghouse. We'd leave at 7 or 7:30 in the morning. Ken didn't get up until 9:30 or 10. We'd all have supper together. Ken went to work 6 days a week, during the afternoon and all evening. He got home after midnight and sometimes I'd see him for just a few minutes or wait up for him but Monday was our night and we'd go out to dinner or to a movie or just someplace and talk.

Given that description, I wonder how much time I actually spent with either my father or with the tall, smiley, blond-haired woman destined to become my next mother during the months that followed? Sometime in the spring—I would guess around Mother's Day—Ruth Ann decided that she would take me to Kansas to meet her family.

In the blink of an eye, as they say, I found myself on a fast-moving passenger train with her, heading away from the stability, comfort and familiarity I had come to know in my grandparents' home. I assume my grandmother must have condoned this trip and probably spoken to me about what to expect on the train, assuring me I would have fun and that I would be okay. It was this trip, however, that gave rise to an incident that would both erode myself image and impact my relationship with my soon to be new mother. The memory has remained consistent and vivid my entire life.

We spent one night on the moving train and the next night in a hotel in some city, Chicago perhaps. It was in that beige and white shaded hotel room that Ruth Ann decided—possibly because she'd overheard my grandmother beginning to teach me the alphabet—that I was surely old enough to recite my ABC's on demand; or, if not, she would tutor me in that performance.

> **I am tired. I miss Nana and Granny, and my daddy. I don't want to be in this strange room. I want to go to sleep . . . I can only say the first few letters. I can't make my brain work the way she wants. She is getting angry. I feel helpless. I want to hide. I am trying hard not to let my tears come but I can't stop them.**

The New (Almost) Mother and Then Another

The longer I was unable to give Ruth Ann what she was demanding of me, the more frustrated she became. Why she thought hitting me across my thighs with a Fuller Brush would elicit what she wanted, I cannot fathom, as both the unexpected action and the stinging pain only made me cry harder. After she used the brush in this way a few times, the monogrammed plate on the back suddenly came loose and fell to the floor. Maybe it startled her into recognizing what she was actually doing. At that point she abandoned her quest and nothing more was said about the ABC's.

The next thing I knew, I was being arranged this way and that for what seemed like endless picture taking with my almost stepmother and various members of her family. Anxious, lonely and sad, I kept quiet, and kept smiling, doing my best to be "a good little girl" as I suspect my father told me to do. Talking nonstop, the woman who was to become his next wife read only the surface, never looking any deeper than my forced, superficial smiles, which, to her, confirmed just the opposite of everything I was feeling. I continued this charade throughout the onslaught of strangers exclaiming how pretty I was and what a sweet smile I had. I ate food I didn't like. I sat in unfamiliar chairs with my back straight, my dangling legs crossed at the ankles, in an effort to emulate my grandmother's posture in social situations. I learned quickly what behavior pleased Ruth Ann. The quicker I smiled, or did whatever she wanted, the more praise she received and the happier she was.

Nearly sixty years into the future, during one of her marathon long distance telephone calls, my mother's mind skipped back decades. As she started reminiscing about the past, I recorded her words:

> I wanted to bring you to Wichita partly to show you off, and partly to prove to myself that you would stay with me, and we came on the train and you never said anything about your Daddy in those four or five weeks and you seemed to be happy and then Ken called and said, 'Guess what? I can get a week off—how fast can you get ready for a wedding?' I about jumped through the phone and anyway, all that time you had never acted like you missed them. We tried to do things to entertain you . . . I was surprised that you didn't seem to miss them but I wanted to see what I could do with you . . .

I now understand that by that point in my life, I had already begun a process called dissociation, a therapeutic term referencing a state of being disconnected from one's thoughts and feelings. When I began to feel helpless, nervous, or scared, I would try to make myself small and invisible so as not to be noticed. I would just energetically disappear and disconnect from my surroundings or a situation that I had no control over. I recognize now that this was a way of protecting myself when feelings of anxiety and fear arose. This coping mechanism followed me into adulthood.

Not yet four years old, I was expected to perform as a flower girl at my father and Ruth Ann's wedding, which took place in a large church sanctuary lavishly decorated with flowers and candles. I have some vague recollection of a rehearsal that must have gone well. When the actual moment arrived, however, with music playing and strangers watching, the aisle seemed overwhelmingly long.

My body freezes. I can't move. Ruth Ann becomes increasingly upset. She tries to push me forward. She hits me hard on my bottom but I still can't move. I am crying. Soon, completely exasperated, she turns her back on me and walks down the aisle.

Was I just left standing there alone? Was anyone else there? Was my crying audible? My grandmother must have figured out what was going on and come and taken me to sit with her.

In the posed wedding photographs, I am standing next to one of the ring bearers who I will become friends with some years later. The basket I'm clutching in my right hand is still filled with rose petals. I am trying, and failing, to force my face into a smile. Studying the photograph today, the most striking thing I notice is how much my face resembles my birth mother's features.

I have no recollection of anything in the hours or days that followed the wedding ceremony. My father and Ruth Ann enjoyed a "grand" honeymoon, described in great detail in her leather-bound vintage memory book, "Our Yesterdays," a wedding gift from her older sister. She recounts activities from movies to stage shows to radio shows to winning money on a last-minute bet at the horse races and "dancing the night away" at various famous night clubs in Kansas City and Chicago. "In the meantime, Nana took Dawn back home so we could be alone."

Was I confused or worried about what was going to happen next, traumatized by the events around the wedding, or was I just relieved to be with my grandparents again in the familiar home I knew and felt safe in?

During another of my mother's long and loquacious telephone calls in the late 1990s, out of the blue she remarked, "I have prayed often for forgiveness . . . even at our wedding I whopped you on the bottom instead of talking to you sweetly and different times when you couldn't learn your ABC's and I probably was a child abuser and didn't know it . . . I didn't know beans about raising a child."

I went into shock momentarily, realizing that she remembered that awful night in the hotel room and then feeling a kind of relief that Mother had come to the awareness she voiced and that she had acknowledged those incidents. Before I could respond, however, she was already chattering on about something else entirely, and I let the moment pass without comment or closure. It was almost as if she forgot I was on the other end of the phone line and was just thinking out loud.

I wonder now when or how she became conscious of the fact that she had done something hurtful to me? Why didn't she ever tell me she was sorry? Did she think I wouldn't remember? Did she have any idea how much those incidents affected our relationship?

According to the copious notes Ruth Ann maintained during the first year of her marriage to my father, "the three of us continued living with his parents for four more months until we moved into a furnished apartment" which I have no memory whatsoever of. Six weeks after that we moved into a new "house with 5 rooms and a full basement." Ruth Ann writes how "swell it is to have a whole house to ourselves and to finally be able to send for and use the wedding gifts to entertain." Regarding Thanksgiving she writes that, "Dawn was in Pittsburgh (at Nana's sister's home) with Nana and Granny from Thursday till Sunday. We had a nice vacation and a big Thanksgiving dinner all alone. Lots of fun for four days!"

Studying a black-and-white photograph of "the brick house on Karen Avenue," which was surrounded by dirt and no landscaping whatsoever, I can access no memory of actually living there, no image of where I slept or what anything looked like inside that house. Though I possess no photographs of the interior of my grandparents' house either, I have distinctly visual memories of parts of the large kitchen: an old treadle sewing machine in one corner that I loved watching my grandmother use; playing under a round wooden table on the black-and-white linoleum floor while she made pancakes, sometimes with blueberries in them; the adjoining dining room, and the drop leaf mahogany table with the pull out drawer lined with green felt to protect the silverware stored between the dividers where Nana and Granny and I sat for dinner every night. I remember sitting next to my grandmother at that same table, enthralled as I watched her needlepoint new covers for the dining room chairs. I remember laying my head in her lap and her brushing my hair, an oft repeated, soothing act that made me feel so loved and cared for that I can never recall that sensation without feeling deep emotion.

Another scene that remains embedded in my memory bank is of kneeling with Nana by a twin bed, with a framed photograph of my father on the side table, in the same room as my crib (the bedroom my father grew up in I now realize) putting my palms together the way Nana did and imitating her words. "Now I lay me down to sleep. I pray the Lord my soul to keep. If I should die before I wake, I pray the Lord my soul to take." This was followed by "God bless Daddy" and "God bless Nana and Granny," etc. I didn't grasp the meaning of all the words at the time of course, yet the intimacy of that repeated ritual created a safe space deep inside me which I later retreated to, repeating the words to myself sometimes when I was alone or lonely in my bed, or when I was missing my grandmother.

I have retained one notable memory from the short time I was living in the new brick house with my father and Ruth Ann.

> **I am in the front seat of a car Ruth Ann is driving holding a large metal pot full of potatoes which someone has just given us. We are going down the steep hill. Without warning, the car door beside me swings open, the metal container on my lap tips, and I see potatoes rolling down the steep hill. I am startled, afraid I am going to fall out of the car and roll down the hill too or crack my head open. Ruth Ann stops the car. She is angry. That means I have done something wrong, but I don't know what . . . She retrieves the pan and a couple of potatoes. She slams my door shut, gets back in her side and finishes the drive in silence. Later I hear Ruth laughing while telling my father and the people who came to dinner about the potatoes rolling down the hill. She says nothing to me or about me, not even that she was relived I didn't fall out of the car. She doesn't seem to even notice that I am in the room. I feel forgotten and invisible.**

There were no seat belts in those days but surely Ruth Ann shut the door on my side of the car. Wouldn't she have gotten me into the seat, then handed me the pot with the potatoes in it and shut the door before going around to her side of the car? Was I supposed to shut the door? How would I have the strength to do that with one arm when I was only three years old? Was she mostly perturbed about losing the potatoes she was going to cook for dinner and I just thought she was mad at me? Was she actually upset with herself for not making sure the door was shut and she projected the blame onto me? Her laughter was likely a deflection.

There was little time to even begin to acclimate to the new house or situation before everything changed again, as Ruth Ann wrote:

May 7, 1948: Ken lost his job at the Latin Quarter.

May 27, 1948: We sold all our furniture during the past 2 weeks & left Cincinnati for good today at 2:00 a.m. headed toward Memphis.

May 28, 1948: Ken left in a plane this morning to join Ted Weems' band in Atlanta.

Years before reading Ruth Ann's notations, I had interviewed my father about his musical career. He said nothing about losing his job, only that he worked at the Latin Quarter nightclub in Newport, Kentucky for about a year and was doing well but growing tired of working so late.

> You'd start around 9 or 10 p.m. and work till 3 or 4 a.m. so you'd end up sleeping all morning. It was while I was playing at the Latin Quarter that a friend of mine came in one day and he was playing with Ted Weems, He said he sure wished he could have a steady job like mine. He was envious of my living at home all the time and not traveling. He was getting tired of the road so I said, 'Well, if you're serious maybe we could trade.' So he gave Ted Weems notice and said he had a replacement. That's when I went with Ted Weems.

Is it possible my father just told Ruth Ann that he'd lost his job rather than saying he wanted the change he described to me? Wouldn't being in a band on the road be the same late hours with the additional stress of travel? Was he just growing bored with staying in one place? Was my existence a consideration at all? Could my father have possibly thought he would go on the road and Ruth Ann would stay behind with me, or did he just assume they would take me with them, but then left the decision up to her because she was now "the mother?"

. . . . .

The first entry from the Children's Home SUMMARY file reads:

> **6-4-48:** Stepmother, Mrs. Kenneth C. Armor came to the Home to make arrangements for placing Dawn, as she wanted to travel with Mr. Armor, who plays with Ted Weems Band and could not take Dawn with them.

Chapter Five
The "Home"

Psychologists and researchers now say that all trauma that occurs . . . from conception to around age five affects brain development as well as identity formation.

—Sandra Pawul

You must find the strength to open the wounds, stick your hands inside, pull out the core of the pain that is holding you in your past, the memories, and make peace with them.

—Iyanla Vanzant

The first typewritten notes in the Children's Home SUMMARY record continues as follows:

> After much consideration and deliberation, the mother's conscience seemed to bother her over leaving the child, finally decided that the Home was the place for her for about one year.

I have no recall relating to the actual move into the Home, though it must surely have been unsettling and confusing. I must have felt powerless as I was forced to adjust to yet another change, and to being left in that huge imposing brick building with no familiar spaces or faces.

The third note in my record is not dated.

> Dawn is quite a sweet child—does not seem to have a sense of security; however, she is not difficult to manage. She gets much pleasure playing with her dolls. She has brown eyes and long hair. Will go to kindergarten this fall.

The irony of the words "does not seem to have a sense of security" is both laughable and depressing to read. My dolls were my only familiar companions in that brand new communal environment. I pretended they were my children, talking to them, kissing them goodnight, and tucking them all in together under a blanket on the small wooden bed my stepmother's brother-in-law had built for me. I "read" to them from the ten by twelve inch hard-boarded, illustrated copy of *The Brimful Book*, given to me the previous year by Nana's sister, my aunt Grace. I guarded that precious gift, that has now been shared with children and grandchildren, the way other young children clutched their teddy bears.

I'm uncertain how many girls were already living in the wing of the building I was placed in. I feel sure I was one of the youngest in the group, although the others were, at most, only a year or two older. A row of simple steel, military style twin beds, maybe ten or twelve, were lined up along each side of the rectangular room with a door that opened to a fire escape at the far end. Not all the beds were filled. The bathroom, and a linoleum-floored, rectangular playroom were near the entrance to this dormitory-like space on one side and the rooms occupied by the woman who was in charge of us were on the other side. My image of Mrs. Hamilton is a tall, pencil thin, old woman with graying hair wrapped into a bun on the back of her head. She had false teeth she kept in a glass by her bed at night, and a harsh demeanor. Whenever one of us cried in response to a rebuke from her, she would shake her finger at the offender, saying, "Stop that crying or I'm going to put you out on the fire escape and you'll freeze that way." The threat was always ominous though I image it worked more quickly as a deterrent during the snowy, Midwestern winters.

On Saturday mornings we had work time after breakfast and before play time because, as Mrs. Hamilton repeatedly reminded us, "Every little girl has to do her work." Each of us was assigned a task, which remained the same every week. Mine was in the bathroom, scrubbing the toilets. Another child cleaned the sinks while I was in the stalls using a cloth rag to make the toilets shine and a scrub brush on the surrounding black-and-white diamond-shaped floor tiles. I remember no other work assignment in the nearly two years I lived in the Home.

Was there any thought put into which child did which job? How were those assignments made? Did we have any choice in the matter? Who did my job on the weekends when I was taken out to visit one of Ruth Ann's relatives? Clearly this work period was simply training for future housewives. There must have been a maintenance staff who did a more thorough cleaning while we were in the dining hall or elsewhere.

My father was on the road with the band that summer playing mostly "one nighters" and writing lengthy, amorous, letters daily to my stepmother who had apparently taken a part-time job in Wichita, presumably to help them out financially. In a letter postmarked June 1, 1948, from Atlanta, GA, my father lists the band's itinerary for the next six weeks. He follows that with a detailed account of money he is sending to his wife, as well as money he has spent before writing:

> I am amazed at the folks' attitude about putting Dawn in a home. Gee honey these are times that get me down. I had just seen the picture "The Mating of Millie"[1] when I read your letter about what to do with Dawn and I felt pretty bad about it. I'm being constantly torn between two principles on the matter, but I guess it will all work out.

I will never know exactly what two principles my father was debating but I am astonished by the naivety in his statement, and by his choice to deny or ignore both his feelings and his responsibilities. I can well imagine how upset my grandparents must have been to discover I was going to be "put into a home," given their intimate experience with the instability of my first few years of life, and their great effort to allay its adverse effects by providing me with security, caring touch, and love during my second year of life.

I remember my grandmother responding to a question I once asked her about how I reacted to leaving their home where I felt safe and pro-

---
1 A romantic comedy that includes a young child living in an orphanage, hoping to be adopted.

tected. She said "Oh you were excited and happy to be with your daddy." She then added that "Your granddad and I felt that it was time for your father to begin to take responsibility for you" and something about feeling that if he didn't take that responsibility then, they were afraid he might never do so.

Had they assumed that my father and my newest stepmother would take me with them on the road when my dad made that decision, hoping perhaps he would find a way to "settle down" by the time I needed to enter school since kindergarten was not mandatory? Could the new information have contributed to my grandfather's "nervous breakdown" I've heard happened around that time?

About ten letters later, my father mentions me again, saying:

> I'm glad your mother and sister went out to the boarding home with you. Their being more satisfied makes me feel better too. Have you said much to Dawn about it? If so, is there any bad reaction? Honest honey I believe I'd just junk this job if I thought Dawn were going to be the least bit unhappy in that home.

What was I told about this move? Did Ruth Ann paint a picture of a happy place with lots of children for me to play with and nice people who would take good care of me? Did she promise I would see her every weekend? Did she truly believe I would be better off living with strangers in another new and different place while she was still living with her parents in the same city? Did I ever consciously think or feel that I was never going to have a real mother, or get to live with my father?

In the same piece of correspondence, my father tells Ruth Ann that he would like it very much if she would plan to be with me on my birthday.

> In my mind I've been thinking about us getting together at the latest in Memphis when we open there the 16th of July but it only seems fair, or rather, it would seem a pity for both of us to be gone on Dawn's birthday when it would only mean a wait of a week or 5 days.

My father ends another letter, saying, "Tell Dawn about everywhere I'm going and give her a big hug and kiss for me."

I wasn't quite four years old. How would it have made any sense to me, or made me feel any better to tell me the names of all the different cities and states my daddy was going to?

In a missive to "Ruthie darling" from Boston, Mass. postmarked June 19, 1948, my father tells his wife how happy he was to receive her Father's Day card and one from me also. "Please thank Dawn for me & tell her Daddy will write her a letter as soon as he gets a chance."

Did Ruth Ann pick out a card for me to send to Daddy for Father's Day? Or did she just buy one and pretend it was from me because she thought it would be cute? Did my father ever write me a letter? Was I told he was going to? If so, did I wait and hope for one that never came?

Several weeks later my father refers to me once again, asking his dearest wife to "Give my love & kisses to Dawn—and don't forget about her honey."

What made me burst into tears reading the words 'don't forget about her honey'? What made Daddy write those words? Maybe she hadn't said anything about me in her letters in a while? Was it possible his conscience was bothering him?

In his letter a few days later, my father mentions my birthday again.

> You didn't say anything about staying in Wichita till after Dawn's birthday—how do you feel about that? In my mind I am planning for you to come & join me in Memphis right after her birthday. Is that OK with you?

He writes about what it's like for him to be playing lead with a good band, detailing how they get back and forth from their jobs, and what he does in his off time. He says he wishes they could find a way to add some pin money while traveling, ending with, "But I think we will make out okay and we'll have a lot of fun."

A note on the back of slightly blurry photo taken on my birthday seems to indicate that perhaps Ruth Ann helped arrange for the party even though, clearly, she wasn't actually there as she had joined my father six days earlier. I don't recognize any of the children in the picture and, unlike my party the previous year, I haven't even a snippet of recall regarding the event.

After all these years, I have several very clear sensory and visual memories from living in the Children's Home. During the first few months I was there, something happened in the playroom one day when we were left unsupervised for a brief time. Two girls got into some sort of tussle over a doll or a toy. The upset escalated, leading to the following scene later that night.

> **We children have nothing on but our bleached white underpanties. We are all being made to walk in a circle in front of the wall of the dark wooden "cubbies" that hold our clean underwear and pajamas. Mrs. Hamilton is pacing back and forth and waving the large red wooden paddle, which usually hangs on a hook on the side of the cubbies. She is demanding one of us tell her what happened but nobody speaks.**

Were we all waiting for someone else to say something, too stressed by the imminent threat of bodily harm, or we were rendered mute by some secret, telepathic choice to remain silent and not "tattle?"

> **Mrs. Hamilton is making us walk faster and faster until we are all almost prancing like little ponies and before long, we are all crying.**

I can't be certain if the paddle was actually used on any one of us that night or if it was simply brandished as an imminent possibility, nor do I remember who or what brought closure to this incident, or how we all made it into our beds.

> **9-7-48 SUMMARY:** Dawn entered kindergarten today. She has developed very much since her arrival in the Home. Is becoming quite plump and is growing noticeably responsive . . .

The "Home"

My memories of anything to do with my first formal school experience are minimal though one in particular has remained vivid, and virtually the same each time I've recalled it. It has to do with the first day of school and a little boy named Gary Troxell whose hair was as white as clean snow. He began crying inconsolably as soon as his mother left. His despair may have eclipsed my own uneasiness, or perhaps I perceived a kindred spirit. What I remember most clearly is that I felt compelled to comfort him. The smiling, dark-haired teacher, who had tried briefly to distract this distraught little boy, had to put her attention on the other parents dropping off their young children. My mission was obvious. I stuck to Gary like glue the rest of the day. He eventually stopped crying though I don't think he ever smiled.

When it came time to roll out our rugs on the polished hardwood floor for quiet time, he and I lay down next to each other. Neither of us went to sleep as some of the other children did. I kept my attention on Gary the entire time. At the end of the nap time, each of us was given a small carton of milk and two graham crackers. I had never liked those hard, dry crackers which I'd encountered before at the Home. I offered mine to Gary. His refusal seemed to increase some unspoken, fragile bond that helped us both survive the first day of being thrown together with strangers in a strange land called kindergarten.

I have recently read studies suggesting that trauma experienced in childhood can increase a person's ability to intuitively understand another person's mental and emotional states, and that this impact is long-standing. In retrospect, I recognize that my sensitivity to loneliness and suffering in others first began to manifest in my encounter with a white-haired, never-to-be-forgotten, little boy, on a sunny September day when I was five years old.

Sometime near the end of that September, during a series of "one nighters" with the band, Ruth Ann was driving while my dad slept after a job. At around 2 a.m., she stopped at a service station to use the bathroom. As she was walking from the restroom back to the car, a drunk driver in a truck came speeding through and hit her. She was thrown up onto the windshield of the truck, shattering the glass and then fell back onto the ground as the driver sped away. My sleeping father was awakened by the sound. He and a couple of men who had witnessed the shocking event managed to get Ruth Ann into the car and to the nearest hospital in the very small town of Rhome, Texas where she was given transfusions, the gash over her eye hurriedly stitched, and a few X-rays taken.

It is unclear how many days Ruth Ann spent in that hospital before my dad was able to get her into a compartment on a train and transferred to a hospital in Wichita. More complete X-rays taken in this larger hospital showed compound skull and sinus fractures. The doctor Ruth Ann later credited as "saving my life" told her it was a miracle that she had lived through her injuries, that she would have to lie quietly on her back for one to two months to heal, and that she could still die.

> **10-6-48** SUMMARY: Mr. Armor came to see Dawn today and take her to Wesley Hospital to visit with her mother. Mrs. Armor met with quite a serious accident when she and Mr. Armor were in Texas. She was brought to Wichita as soon as she was able to travel.

I have a vague impression of being in a hospital room and seeing Ruth Ann. One of her eyes was swollen shut and her hair was all matted. I remember her saying that they couldn't comb her hair because she had so many cuts on her head. I think the visit was brief, probably so as not to tire her. I have no idea how much time, if any, I may have spent with my father before it was time to say goodbye to him again when he took me back to the Home that day.

I feel such sadness just thinking about what it might have been like to see Daddy again for what must have been a very short time, wondering how it was for him, or what I must have felt when he brought me back to the home. Did I cry when he left or just bury my feelings?

My father sent tenderly affectionate and encouraging letters to Ruth Ann daily. They reveal that she was finally allowed to sit up for five minutes at a time and write a few lines to my father. Her handwriting in the short letters during that week, is uneven and childlike. One letter begins with her apologizing for her selfishness and promising she will do better. In another, she seems to be going through some sort of mental crisis.

> Darling, I want another chance to prove to you that I can be a

The "Home"

good wife. I'm afraid I had grown into a griping, nagging person. My conscience seems to bother me so. Someday when I am well, you & Dawn & I will be together again. I do love her. I'm sorry I said such awful things about her.

Did this uncharacteristic expression come from a drugged state? What awful things had she said? When did she say them? Was this another reason she made the decision to take me to live in the Children's Home? Did she think they would somehow shape me into being a "good little girl" or one that she'd be better able to manage?

By the end of October, her letters reveal that Ruth Ann was able to get out of bed and take a few steps before being released to her parents' home to continue her bed rest, recovery and rehabilitation process. In a letter written after I was brought to see her, she writes about me giving them all a synopsis of a play that the children from the Home were taken to see and how detailed it was. She then reiterates that she loves me now, saying she felt it was a duty or obligation before, but that now she actually feels she loves me.

In a letter dated Nov. 4, 1948 my father reassures Ruth Ann that he has everything planned out and asks her again not to worry about her condition, to have faith in her doctor. Towards the end of the letter, he assures her that no matter what happens he loves her, saying that is "something in me to stay."

> It wouldn't make any difference if you came back to me with one eye, a wooden leg and flat feet. Now don't cry sweetheart, just be happy and have nice thoughts . . .

In one of his daily letters a few weeks later my father urges his wife, yet again, to take good care of herself.

> Please don't do anything that will retard your recuperation baby. Make sure to eat lots and just think about the future. And remember that everything will work itself out OK.

As she begins writing longer letters to my father, Ruth Ann's cognitive abilities seem to improve, and her determined and directive personality reasserts itself. Even though my father pleads with her to let him take care of things and to just concentrate on getting her strength back, she begins giving him explicit suggestions on everything from how to deal with the bills and the insurance company to how to make some extra money selling the Christmas cards they had apparently already purchased and planned to resell for a profit. His letter recounts how busy he is, rehearsing, working, getting their car in shape and fixing up their trailer in preparation for her return.

A few weeks later Ruth Ann is still harping on the card selling, pointing out various ways for my father to sell them door to door. She returns to the theme at the end of still another letter, mentioning to her husband that he is so handsome, no one will be able to refuse buying cards from him. He continues to give her updates on his daily activities, including everything he does on his days off, how much money he is spending on specific items and urging her not to try to do too much too soon. At that time, the band had been playing for an extended period of time at the Aragon Ballroom on Lick Pier in Santa Monica and my father broaches the possibility of Ruth Ann bringing me with her when she is able to rejoin him. She responds by saying:

> For the first time, I can truthfully say I want to but I don't believe it would be best. She is well adjusted here & seems satisfied . . . I really think some of this has been good for her. She seems much better behaved than when I had her . . . It will be different when I have her again, honey I will have better luck now, because I now love her & want to have her. Before I didn't want her, I just thought I had to do it, but my heart wasn't into it . . . I can see how wrong I was. But I don't see how I could manage. There would be so much noise and work to do, extra washing, etc. When I come to you, I shan't be really well. So, don't have your hopes too high. I do want her though . . . but sickness and a child and such a small trailer. Do you think I should?

Throughout her lifetime, Ruth Ann had a way of saying things that made it clear she wasn't really asking a question; she was, rather, pointing out the other person's flawed logic. If someone disagreed with her, or presented a different point of view, she would just keep talking and saying the same thing over and over again, perhaps in some slightly different way

The "Home"

until the person who couldn't get a word in edgewise simply gave in to whatever she was wanting.

Was that something she did consciously? Was she even aware of what she was doing and of the effect it had on the other person? Did anyone ever try to point it out to her? Where did she learn that? I don't remember her mother, or either of her sisters ever speaking that way.

My father continued to write detailed and romantic letters to Ruth Ann while her letters become more and more specifically directive, particularly in regard to their finances. "Are you writing all your expenses down? Please do." In one of his letters, my father pleads again with his wife not to worry about things or do anything that might slow down her recuperation. He asks her again to let him handle the hospital bills.

> A husband is responsible for his wife's bills, & if I don't want to pay them what they say—it's up to them to contact me, not you. If they want to know anything you tell them to just take it up with me.

She writes back telling him she can't forget the hospital bills and basically disagreeing with the way he wants to handle things. It becomes obvious that telling her not to worry or think about money is like telling a zebra it doesn't have stripes. She went ahead and argued with the hospital about the bill and contacted the insurance company.

My father proposes to sell their Mercury. She objects. He proposes they sell the trailer, laying out why it would ultimately save them money. Ruth Ann counters with her own logic. My father gets a speeding ticket and a $50 fine. He apologizes, asking his wife to please not be "too disgusted with me" and saying he really wasn't exceeding the limit that much.

Ruth Ann lost her long, blond hair after the accident and was unable to bleach what she had left. She writes my father describing various styles for her short, dark hair, making jokes about how she may look now. It seems fairly obvious that she is using humor as a cover for her worry about appearing less attractive to my father and to other people. My father writes that her hair style is not what is important to him and to just concentrate on getting her strength back.

By mid-December, Ruth Ann is thinking about clothing she now needs, informing my father it will cost less to buy some before coming to California and asking if my he can send her some money. She tells him how many Christmas cards she has sold and urges him, once more, to please try to sell some of the cards. She reminds him to keep them in his car so they are handy, ending with, "Let me know if you have tried."

When my father sends a clipping about a specific kind of doll that he thinks I might like as a Christmas present, Ruth Ann writes back describing the several dolls I already have before saying, "Do you think we should give her another doll? Don't you believe she would enjoy other things more? Next year maybe she will need a new dolly—do you agree?"

Clearly Daddy backed down at that point and deferred to her on the matter. Was it because he really thought she was right, because he didn't want to belabor the issue, or was he was too weak-willed to pursue a different point of view?

These lengthy pieces of correspondence between Ruth Ann and my father point to certain patterns, especially in relationship to money, that will contribute to the disintegration of their relationship less than a decade later.

As the holidays approach, my father asks his wife:

> How do they handle the Christmas situation where Dawn is? I do hope Santa remains Santa. Dawn should keep thinking that for a couple years yet . . . Honey do you tell Dawn that we're all going to be together soon? Honest honey, I don't want to put that off long regardless.

And yet I spent another school year living in the Children's home. Daddy didn't quit the band until late summer of 1950.

Ruth Ann responds to some of my father's questions while ignoring others and seems to be doing her best to convince my father of the perfectly wonderful time I am going to have during the Christmas holidays.

> I spoke with the supervisor and they are getting candy, gifts and everything . . . they will have a party most every night out there

The "Home"

next week . . . Yes, Dawn still believes in Santa. Either Fern or Mama will have her one Christmas day . . . This will be a Christmas for her to remember!

Did she say that because she thought all kids at that age cared about at Christmas time is how many gifts they receive? Did I have feelings knowing she was leaving to go be with my daddy but I didn't get to go, or had I just given up hoping or wishing for such things?

In her next missive, Ruth Ann expresses great disappointment that my father has been unable to get leave from the band to fly back to Wichita for Christmas and to accompany her on the return trip. She laments the fact that he won't get to meet her sister's new baby before telling my father that he should have approached the matter in a different way. Weems had apparently not taken my father's request well, and recommended that he hire a nurse to be with his wife on the train.

Daddy responds to her comment with a hint of irritation, as well as relief that he needn't be concerned about my having a good Christmas without him or his wife.

Yes, it is too bad I won't see Doris's baby, but after all I won't even get to see Dawn . . . I'm so glad to hear you say that her Christmas will be a nice one.

When my father urges Ruth Ann, once again, to fly to California, she writes that she will be arriving at the LA train station the morning of Dec. 23rd. "To tell the truth I'm scared to death to ride a plane now. I guess the accident did that to me, so I'll come by train." My dad's reply included a comment about how odd it was that her accident made her afraid to fly since there was no plane involved, before assuring her that he will take his alarm clock and sleep overnight at the depot, to make sure he is there in plenty of time to greet her.

Other than going to a circus performance for the first time in my life, and being completely mesmerized by the trapeze artists and tight rope walkers, I can access no memories at all regarding that Christmas season, either at the Children's Home or with Ruth Ann's relatives.

. . . . .

I'm unsure at what point during my stay in the Home the following incident took place. The scene, however, has remained indelibly etched in my mind.

> **The tall skinny girl with the straight light-blond hair is tied to her bed with strips of sheets. She is on her back. Her arms are stretched above her head, each one tied at the wrist to one side of the bars that form the bed's head frame. Her legs are separated so that one ankle is tied to each side of the bottom of the bed frame. I feel so bad for her. I feel scared. She isn't crying or moving. What did she do wrong? Why is she being punished like that? I feel sad. I look away and try to pretend I don't really see her.**

Is it possible that being tied to her bed was an intervention meant to cure sleep walking? Or did she try sneak out of the building in the middle of the night? I think she was in the Home, or at least in the section I was in, for only a brief period. Every time I remember that girl and that scene replays itself in my mind, I wonder where she might have been sent and why.

Another lucid memory from my time living in the Children's Home that has stayed with me, began as a punishment—for what I have no idea—yet it turned out to be a prescient experience.

> **I am in the last bed at the end of the dormitory, past several empty beds, next to the fire escape. This isolation is how Mrs. Hamilton punishes any of us who have done something she deems unacceptable. I am having trouble getting to sleep in the bed without my dolls next to me, but I don't feel afraid, just a little more alone than usual. I am looking out of the high window when I hear a voice coming out of the moon just as a cloud passes over it. I decide it must be God. The voice is comforting somehow and I feel less alone. It feels as if I now have a secret protector.**

Although the exact words I heard that night disappeared long ago, I've never forgotten the essence of the event. In hindsight, I recognize that this was my first spiritual—or what some would call mystical—experience, in terms of making a connection to something outside myself

The "Home"

and feeling I was not alone.

According to the Children's Home medical records, I had the chicken pox in January of 1949. The most impactful visual and sense memory I retain from living in the Children's Home occurred during that month. Ruth Ann was in Wichita to have some dental work done related to her accident and head injuries.

> **I'm wearing my warm, yellow, footed pajamas, alone in the second-floor dormitory room with only my dolls for company. All the other children and are in the dining room eating lunch. In the chicken pox outbreak, I was the last one in my section to have a pox detected during the daily inspections. An older girl comes in with a tray of food for me. She tells me I am going to have a visitor soon and quickly leaves. I don't feel hungry. I don't know who is coming to see me . . . She walks into the room and sits down on the bed next to mine. She is wearing a full-length coat with a fur collar. Smiling at first, she starts talking right away. I can't think of what to say, and she's talking so fast I don't have time to think. I wish my daddy was here instead of her. She doesn't touch me. Maybe she is afraid of getting the chicken pox? Her smile fades and she is looking at me as if I've done something wrong. She's upset. I am trying not to cry. My stepmother says, "Well, if you aren't going to talk to me, I might as well leave." I can't think fast enough of something to say. As she walks out of the room, my tears spill out. I get out of bed and hurry toward the doors leading out to the hallway. I make my way down the wide polished wooden stairs, all by myself, as fast as I can. When I reach the bottom, I hear voices from the dining room but there is no one in the hallway. I arrive at the tall, double doors with glass in the top half. I try to open one of the doors but it doesn't budge. On my tiptoes, I can see her walking toward the taxi cab at the end of the long sidewalk. I want her to turn around and see me. I open my mouth to call, 'please don't leave. I'm sorry, please come back,' but no sound comes out. She gets in the cab. It pulls away from the curb and disappears. I slowly walk back through the hallway and climb the stairs. I crawl back into my bed and curl up inside myself.**

The taxi was clearly waiting curbside, and Ruth Ann didn't even take off her coat. She couldn't have been planning to stay much longer than a few minutes with me that day in any case! Did she just come so she could tell my father that she had seen me? What did she tell him about that visit?

That scene has replayed itself in my mind many times across the years. While writing about it, my entire body began convulsing with silent sobs that seemed endless. I found myself on my feet kicking and punching the air with my fists, my breath spewing out in howls and growls. It wasn't so much rage that erupted in me but an experience of power unleashed. My energy filled the room around me and the space outside my window.

. . . . .

> May 17, 1949: DISMISSED to her father and mother. They thought she could go with them in their trailer and have a wonderful summer.

Studying a photograph of my father standing in front of the mini mobile home he often referred to as the "blather" for reasons I've yet to figure out, it seems barely big enough for two people, let alone a third. I have no idea where I slept inside the trailer or any image whatsoever of the inside.

I do retain a collage of impressions from life in the trailer park: the ice man who drove into the open space in the middle of the area once a week or so, opened the door of his truck, and picked up huge blocks of ice with a big tong-like utensil to carry them to various recipients; my dad's tall and cheerful whistling friend, who I would eventually figure out was Elmo Tanner, the well-known "Whistling Troubadour" and singer featured on a number of records with the Ted Weems Orchestra. He helped my dad improve his whistling skills and had a son near my age, "Little Elmo," whom I often played with.

The most memorable incident from that summer unfolded when my father took me to the ocean—actually the Galveston Bay along the

The "Home"

Gulf of Mexico. When I was reluctant to walk into the water, he put me on his shoulders. The sea water was nearly up to his chest when he tripped on something and we both went down. Although it was surely only a matter of seconds before my father pulled me up and out of the water, flailing and coughing, the shock, compounded a couple summers later by another water-related trauma, had repercussions for years to come.

. . . . .

> RE-ENTERED 9-6-49: Mrs. Armor returned Dawn to the Home for the school year . . . she had a grand time going with her parents in the trailer.

Did the person making these notes actually talk with me about my summer, or did Ruth Ann simply wax eloquent about what a great time I had? Did I really readjust instantly to the change back to living in the Children's Home? I have no memory of the actual transition.

In a two-column article in the Women's Activities Section of a San Francisco newspaper, for Sunday, Oct. 30, 1949, the headline reads: **"The Band Plays On** . . . and the Orchestra Wives Keep Electric Plates Burning." There are two large photos. One of the photos is of three women and two children, both four years old. The second photo, captioned "Gin rummy while the band rehearses" shows Ruth Ann sitting in the foreground at a table with another woman. The article states that, "The Armors had a red brick house in Cincinnati; sold it and their furniture for a chance to travel." It states that "the wife of Elmo Tanner, the whistler, was not present that day as she was picking up Little Elmo, age 6, from school." A bit further down in the article, this line appears: "Mrs. Armor's daughter, Dawn, was an orchestra child, too, until she had to enter school this fall. She lives with her maternal grandmother in Wichita."

I can visualize Ruth Ann in the interview, chiming in with this misinformation. Her conscience must have still been bothering her in regard to leaving me behind and placing me in a residential institution. Maybe she couldn't admit, even to herself, that she wanted more time alone with my father without having to take care of a young child she barely knew.

A much smaller article that appeared in Ruth Ann's hometown newspaper a couple of months later, states that, "Ruth Ann and her husband Ken Armor are having a grand time touring the country in their luxury trailer with the Ted Weems Orchestra."

I have few recollections from my first-grade school year beyond a long-lingering and pleasurable sense memory of learning to print letters, carefully forming a capital A followed by a small a and so on. I loved performing this practice on the special paper we were given for that purpose with a top and bottom base line and a broken line in the middle. By the end of the year, along with the delight of learning how to read, we were practicing writing in cursive which was even more exciting than block letters.

The records I requested and received from the Children's Home some sixty years after the two years I lived there, included the report card from my first year in an elementary school named after the woman who wrote one of my favorite books—read under my bedcovers with a flashlight far into the night some years later—Louisa May Alcott. On the last page, in the space for the quarterly notes, my first-grade teacher writes that I am above my grade level in reading and writing, before stating, "Dawn needs to get books from the City Library and read aloud this summer to keep up speed and increase eye span." City libraries were not in my foreseeable future. However, my grandmother's interest in books and, eventually, school libraries, helped support and sustain my passion for reading.

> The last entry in my Children's Home SUMMARY reads **5-26-50** DISMISSED: Dawn is going with her parents traveling over the country.

I actually spent the better part of that summer, including my 7th birthday, in the security and warm embrace of my grandparents in Charlotte, North Carolina where they were living for a short time. My grandmother didn't continually cuddle or coddle me; yet I always felt unconditionally embraced and loved by her. I knew I could trust her. I could let my guard down and be myself.

My father left Ted Weems sometime in August of 1950. Forty years later I asked him what prompted his decision to quit at that particular time.

The "Home"

Well, each month I sort of got a little more worn out from being on the road all the time, plus I felt it was a young man's business and not conducive to having a family . . . I had a need to settle down gnawing at me you could say. I had a little girl and you weren't supposed to go traveling around with a baby girl.

Chapter Six

A Few (Nearly) Normal Years

A single image can split open the hard seed of the past and soon memories pour forth from every direction.
—Mary Kerr

We ache all our lives to be loved unconditionally, to be seen as we truly are, without judgement . . . held in that vast cherishing and acceptance.
—Jan Frazier

When my father left his job with the Ted Weems Orchestra, he and I and my stepmother, Ruth Ann, stayed with her parents for a short time. The day before I was to begin second grade, my father drove me through the route I would walk to the school I'd be attending. The next morning, I was nervous and worried that I wouldn't remember the way, yet I seemed to have no choice but to start walking. I didn't notice any other kids, but a few blocks into the walk, my heart began to pound when a large, long-haired dog seemed to appear out of nowhere and began moving in my direction. Having had little to no experience with any canines at that point in my life, I didn't know what to do.

The closer the dog came, the more uneasy I felt. I was frozen in my tracks when, to my incredible relief, my father appeared! He had been slowly following me in his car to make certain I got to the school okay. He showed me how to hold the back of my hand out for the dog to sniff. He wasn't the least bit nervous and started petting the dog. I worked up my courage enough to follow his example. Then he smiled at me, told me to get into the car, and drove me to the school.

I remember how safe and happy it made me feel to know that my father had been watching me, and how grateful I was to see him. On that day my father became the man my grandmother had always told me he was, as she assured me that I would be with him someday. He became my hero. I felt claimed by him at last.

I recall nothing about the school itself, which I only attended for a week or two. Since I don't remember ever walking all the way to the school, I am guessing that my father decided to drive me there each day and then stopped somewhere to have coffee and some time to himself, and probably to search the want ads for jobs.

We soon moved into a housing development known as Hilltop Manor, which was built originally by the federal government during the war to house defense workers and their families. After the war ended, the units were sold to a Residential Housing Association, and another 400 of these back-to-back, four-room dwellings were added a few years later.

My father and I spent a lot of time together during the next couple of years. He had started playing golf, often with one of my new uncles, and I happily went with him to the course whenever I got the chance. He gave me a nickel for every stray ball I found and taught me how to use the crank-style ball washing machines, though I never developed an interest in learning how to play the game itself. We dyed Easter eggs, decorated the Christmas tree in the same way his parents had, with ornaments he inherited from them, and he tutored me in the use of firecrackers, "worms," and sparklers on the 4th of July. Maybe he was experiencing some regret or guilt about having missed so much of my life up to that point and was making up for lost time, or maybe he really liked being a father, or perhaps it was some of both. Interviewing him not long before his death, I asked if it had been difficult for him to give up playing music professionally.

> Ken:
> Sure. When I left Ted Weems and moved to Wichita, the feeling was that I would not be in the music business anymore because no one would know me there. Funny thing was that one of the first people I met in Wichita was a musician who had been in the same place I was in Florida when I was down there on R and R. He had his own band in Wichita and wanted to use me on weekends and for things like Broadway shows that came to town—*Hello Dolly* was one—the Shrine Circus, and so on, and of course on New Year's Eve.

Dawn:
I remember you taking me with you when you played for the Ice Capades and the Circus. You turned your saxophone case on its end for me to sit on, so I could be right next to you in the front corner of the bandstand. I had a great view!

Ken:
I also played at the Sims Park in Riverside for their summer concert series.

Dawn:
I remember! In the Gazebo! Why did you stop those jobs?

Ken:
Well, it got to the point where I just wanted to get rid of everything because if I didn't, I would end up going out on the road again, since most of the music business involved traveling unless you lived in a large major city. Ruth wanted to be in Wichita.

In 1947, my stepmother wrote the following underneath the heading, "My Greatest Ambition," on the page entitled "Wife's Personal Record," in a special book she and my father had received as a wedding gift: "I used to want to be a model. Now that I am married, my greatest ambition would be to be an ideal housewife and mother." The dozens of photographs of Ruth Ann, posing as if she was a fashion model, around the time she met my father, are obvious proof of her modeling aspirations (and certainly indicative of her lifelong obsession with posing herself and others for endless snapshots). She would later say more than once that her mother had forbidden her modeling ambition. Whether Ruth Ann actually believed what she wrote about  wanting to be an ideal housewife and mother, or she thought that saying so would please my father, it was not the way her life would unfold.

A Few (Nearly) Normal Years

In Wichita, Ruth Ann had immediately procured a door-to-door sales job working for a photographer. She not only set up in-home appointments but got to go with the photographer to pose people for their portraits. She later sold Tupperware for a while before becoming a top salesperson for Encyclopedia Britannica. I am certain her success at selling things was due to her tenacity and persistence in the art of persuasion. I am also certain that some people purchased whatever she might be selling in order to get her to stop talking.

Sometime during that first year of our settling in as a family, Ruth Ann was persuaded to join her younger sister and their mother in becoming a member of a conservative, non-denominational church they had been attending. She and I then began going to the same church every Sunday morning, Sunday night, and, eventually, Wednesday nights as well. My father and uncle did not share this interest, but my two younger cousins and I had no choice in the matter.

I mostly daydreamed during the sermon part of the church services for the next few years, though I loved the singing. Since no musical instruments were used, the entire congregation sang together in four-part harmony. Ruth Ann loved to sing and she had a beautiful soprano voice. This shared experience brought us closer for a time and led to my involvement in choral singing through the next decade and beyond.

. . . . .

My father was not around the night a never-to-be-forgotten trauma-laden incident occurred.

> **I am eight years old, sitting at our kitchen table in our Hilltop Manor duplex, eating a bowl of canned peaches after some sort of short altercation with my stepmother in which I had disagreed with her. She walks into the kitchen and tells me, in a steely voice, that she is leaving me home alone while she goes to church that night because I "sassed" her.**

Did she really think missing a Wednesday night, hour-long church service was an effective punishment, or did she actually have some idea of how afraid I was of being left alone in the dark at night and therefore feel it was the best way to discipline me in order to make sure I would never again disagree with anything she might say?

> As soon as she leaves, I begin feeling uneasy. The darker it gets the more anxious I become. I get the idea to call the kind woman who I stayed with during the week days the previous summer. When she answers her phone, I tell her I am alone and admit I am scared. She quickly assures me that she will be right over and arrives within minutes pulling the weathered red wagon I am familiar with. She tells me to get in the wagon and we quickly cross the grassy field between our units to the duplex just like ours, where she is raising eight boys whose names I had memorized from the oldest to the youngest: Joe, Tony, Pat, Chris, Jackie, Bede, David and Ray. I have never been in this crowded dwelling at night, nor have I ever seen the boys' father. When we arrive, one of the older boys pulls a younger brother onto his lap to make room for me to sit at the already crowded table. I watch, fascinated, as the strong and sturdy looking Mr. Crawley moves his fingers over a long string of beads with a pretty little gold cross dangling from bottom, while everyone else, except the youngest children, repeat the same words and over. I am surprised to see these often loud, rowdy boys so clean and calm. As this unusual comes to an end, Mrs. Crawley takes me into one of the two bedrooms where I quickly fall asleep on the big bed next to the baby in his crib.

I assume Mrs. Crawley must have left a note for my parents before taking me to her house that memorable night. I have no way of knowing what words might have been exchanged when my stepmother came to get me—whether she was grateful, angry, or embarrassed. I was certain she would be mad at me, but the matter was never mentioned.

By third grade, I was a "latchkey kid," which meant I was alone each school day for a little over two hours before either of my parents got home. We didn't have a television or even a radio yet at that time. Ruth Ann gave me chores to do each day which included emptying and cleaning all the ashtrays and hand-washing my father's dirty socks. The tasks didn't take that long, and eight-year-olds did not have homework in those days. In good weather, I sometimes sat outside on the porch steps playing with a young cat that came around, or rode the secondhand red scooter my father had gotten somewhere and brought home for me.

This was my first venture into duplicity, since I had been instructed not to go out of the house during that time. The following year I sometimes lingered on the playground after school, practicing hanging by both knees or doing one-knee turnovers on the parallel bars. This minor deceit was never discovered and, for the first time, I began to feel I had some small amount of control over my own life.

I was getting close to nine years old when something transpired that paralleled the traumatic ABC's incident in the hotel room five years earlier.

> **We are standing at a bus stop on a busy street in the middle of town. Ruth Ann is trying to teach me the street names and have me explain which ones are parallel and which ones intersect. She keeps giving me information and asking me to repeat it. When I am unable to do what she wants, she becomes progressively cross. My stomach starts to hurt. The bus stops for us but she waves it on. It is getting dark. She begins again, declaring in her slightly louder, irritated voice, "Douglas Street runs east to west." I don't really know which way is east and which is west, but I can repeat what she says. She names another street and ask me which way it runs. I can't tell her. The bus stops again and she waves it on again. She then insists that we are not going home until I can repeat back to her whatever it is that she wants me to learn. I can't hold back my tears. I feel smaller and smaller. The sky has darkened. I am cold. The third time the bus stops, she gives me a quick push and we get on. She keeps talking on the bus but I've gone somewhere else, deep inside myself, and I can't hear her.**

I wish I had been born with as innate a sense of direction and the navigational skills my stepmother obviously possessed. Decades would pass before I would learn that I was directionally challenged, a condition sometimes referred to as spatial or geographic dyslexia. This affliction is distinguished by a tendency to become disoriented or easily lost and, for some people (like myself) having difficulty retracing directions or reading maps. Many, many other people in the world have this challenge to one degree or another. I simply do not have an inner compass. To this day, I emerge from a building or elevator and nearly always start to turn in the exact opposite direction of the one I need to be heading in.

By the time I was nine, my stepmother decided I should be seeing a dentist. Getting to the dentist's office required a bus trip into town, transferring to another bus and then remembering where to get off. Once I stepped off the bus, I needed to walk a few blocks to a tall building, find the elevator once inside, get off on the correct floor, and locate the dentist's office. It was an excursion I always dreaded.

Surely Mother must have gone with me at least once to show me the steps to getting there and to introduce me to the dentist. Did she do such things all by herself when she was a child? She obviously had no trouble with directions and she seemed to be a spirited person willing to try new things without any fear of failure. Clearly, she simply had no context for understanding how difficult and anxiety producing this particular task was for me.

With or without a parent in the waiting room, I suspect almost any person of my generation has less-than-happy memories about their early dental experiences.

> **A pretty, dark-haired lady tells me her name is June and helps me step onto a stool and into the huge black chair. As she clips a giant white paper bib onto my clothing, she smiles as if to reassure me that I will be okay. A gray-haired man in a white jacket and big glasses appears. He speaks to June in muted, short words, though never to me. When June places big clear goggles on my face, they soon become spattered with various materials so I can't really see much even if I open my eyes. I feel trapped.**

The rubber-rimmed mask that was sometimes placed over my whole face was even more disquieting and made me feel woozy and weird. Once released from the mask or the goggles, after the endless mouth rinsing with cold water, spitting into the porcelain miniature basin yet again, and having the paper bib removed before being helped out of the chair, I would be given a little note which I was told to exchange it for ice cream in the drugstore on the first floor.

I felt incredibly small reaching my arm up to hand the paper to the man behind the counter. Once he noticed me, and figured out that I wasn't attached to an adult, the note was quickly exchanged for a frozen fudge bar. I could only tarry so long in the drugstore or standing outside, feeling self-conscious and conspicuous while trying to eat an ice-cold chocolate bar that I didn't particularly like before figuring out how to dispose of the wrapper and stick before beginning my return journey.

This entire ordeal became only slightly easier as I grew older. Even in adulthood, many years would pass before I was able to show up, on time, for any dental appointment, whether it was for a routine cleaning, a filling, a tooth extraction or a root canal, without a great deal of anxiety.

That summer, without asking my opinion in the matter, Ruth Ann signed me up for viola lessons, which required an even longer bus trip across town. After a few days, having found no comfort or inspiration in the small class, I decided to skip it entirely. Instead of transferring to the second bus, I ventured into the big Woolworth's store on that particular corner, got myself onto one of the red bar stools at the counter, and ordered a 19-cent vanilla malt. It took some time, using the straw provided, to finish this sweet, thick concoction, which arrived in a big, stainless steel container that would fill the footed, V-shaped glass it came in nearly twice. After slowly consuming this satisfying beverage, I'd sometimes wander around Woolworth's by myself as my malted shake settled, before getting on the bus and going home. The young man teaching the class eventually contacted my stepmother and my deception was discovered. I believe this was the line I crossed which led to the first "belt episode" punishment.

I will never know how my stepmother made her decisions in regard to the disciplinary methods she chose for me or if she ever read Dr. Benjamin Spock's book advising parental affection over corporal punishment. What is clear is that my father seemed to relinquish any responsibility in the matter, leaving such things entirely up to his wife.

The first time my father took me into my bedroom, shut the door, removed his leather belt and told me he was going to have to punish me, I had no idea what was happening. I cried as much from the shock of my father's actions as from the stinging pain of the belt strap against my bare skin. The next time this occurred, I was forewarned after overhearing my stepmother declaring emphatically, "you have to use the belt!" My dad prefaced the wallops by saying rather sadly, "This hurts me as much as it does you." The hard thwack of leather on my thighs was just as startling though it seemed to me that my father might be using a little less force than he had before. I cried louder thinking maybe it would make the ordeal end more quickly. After the belt whippings stopped, I convinced myself it was because my father refused to keep doing such a horrible thing.

When Ruth Ann's job occasionally took her out of town overnight, I was thrilled to have time alone with my father. Ruth Ann had taught me how to prepare a meal on such occasions: put two Russet potatoes in the oven to bake for one hour; fashion two round "patties" from ground beef and fry them on both sides; and boil some frozen peas. On such nights, after he helped me clean up the dishes, my dad would set up a little table and some folding chairs outside under a big oak tree when the weather was nice enough, so we could play games. He taught me how to play Chinese Checkers and introduced me to Scrabble, which became a lifelong pleasure, though it would be a long time before I even came close to my dad's high scores. When it was my bedtime, he always tucked me in and kissed me goodnight.

I had grown used to calling out to my father in the middle of the night when I had what I'd been told were "growing pains" in my legs. He never failed to come and massage my legs until I fell back asleep. A keen memory of a night when my stepmother was away and he didn't respond when I called has never left me.

> **I keep calling louder and louder, but Daddy doesn't come. I finally get out of bed to search for him but can't find him anywhere. The light is on in the living room where I see several bed pillows in the corner piled up on top of the telephone. I don't understand. I begin to feel nervous and uneasy. I decide to call my Aunt Fern who tells me not to worry, that she and my uncle will come right over.**

When my father returned not long after they had arrived, he explained that he'd gone to his musician friend's house to play poker, and had covered our new, corded telephone so that it wouldn't wake me if it rang. He said he hadn't been gone very long.

Did my aunt ever say anything to my mother about that night? Was my father embarrassed to find his brother- and sister-in-law at our house when he came home? Did he tell his wife what happened? Did she think it was fine for him to leave me alone? Did it ever even occur to either of them that I might be afraid of being left alone in the dark at night given what had transpired during my first year of life?

· · · · ·

The summer I turned ten, we moved into a three-bedroom brick home in a new housing development. The house had a small screened in porch and a big back yard. I got to help pick out the wallpaper that would go on one wall my bedroom. Someone loaned us an upright piano and my dream of taking piano lessons came true for a short while.

I was shy at my new school at first. I preferred to consume my lunch—a baloney and American cheese on white bread with mayonnaise sandwich, a small bag of potato chips and some kind of store-bought cookie—as slowly as I could, while reading, instead of joining the other kids outside. In time, I was lured onto the playground by Double Dutch jump ropes, and discovered I was also good at tether ball. "Red Rover, Red Rover" became my favorite game because I could run fast and hard and I was good at changing directions at the last second to break through.

Ruth Ann's younger sister and family lived only a couple of blocks away from us in their own new house and we spent lots of time with them, especially during the summer months. Possibly because they got a television set before we did, or perhaps because theirs was bigger, we often walked over to their house to watch TV shows like *I Love Lucy*, *Ozzie and Harriet*, or *Father Knows Best*. My cousins and I sat on the floor in front of the television, eating freshly popped corn drizzled with melted butter and drinking Pepsi out of colored aluminum tumblers.

I began to feel comfortable calling Ruth Ann "Mother." My two cousins felt more like a younger sister and brother. During extended warm weather holidays, we three kids helped make homemade ice cream by taking turns cranking my uncle's wooden ice-cream maker handle until it required adult strength to continue. We devoured the ice cream, after the mid-afternoon barbecues, along with generous pieces of my aunt's famously delicious homemade peach pies. We gleefully watched the aerial fireworks display together on July 4th, and went to drive-in movies together, parking our cars in side-by-side slots, sometimes with a space in between for lawn chairs and blankets. My life began to feel predictable and safe.

A distant echo floats back to me—the laughter of children playing tag in the twilight.

> **I am one of the children. We are chasing each other around on sweet-smelling, freshly-mowed grass, giggling and carefree, as we try to catch lightning bugs to hold in our cupped hands for a minute or two. My legs are strong, my skin tanned "brown as a berry," as Daddy always said.**

Ruth Ann's older sister and her husband had no children of their own, whether by choice or by chance I never knew. They gave each of us kids thoughtful and unique gifts for Christmas, Easter and our birthdays, and surprise treats like spending the night at their house or taking us on special outings. Since their house had a basement, the extended family gathered there when tornado warnings got bad enough. My cousins and I played "quiet tag" or hide and seek while the grownups listened to the radio and played card games around a table in the southwest corner. We all spent Christmas Eve at their house every year, and watched the New Year's Day parade there also. After the parade, the three sisters habitually retreated to the kitchen while the men watched the football game, and we cousins entertained ourselves in various ways.

. . . . .

A few weeks after my eleventh birthday, I sensed something was amiss when my father wasn't home on Saturday morning and a Western Union telegram was delivered. My mother read it and said nothing though her energy and demeanor quickly changed. She seemed preoccupied and distracted. Another knock on the front door brought a Special Delivery letter that night. The minute Mother left for work Monday morning, I quickly found the telegram, which simply read: "SPECIAL DELIVERY LETTER WILL REACH YOU EARLY THIS EVENING LOVE KENNETH."

The typewritten letter began, "Dear Ruth…"

There comes a time when a person has got to do what they feel

> they must do. I would rather cut off my arm than do what I'm about to but that wouldn't help. I am leaving Wichita. I realize this will put many hardships on your shoulders and that I am causing a great deal of suffering but if I stay there seems no hope for me. I want to get away by myself and try to grow up again . . . I must start from scratch and by myself. As for Dawn, I think the only thing to tell her is the truth, that I have gone to try and get a fresh start.

Reading the letter, all I could think of was that my father had left me, and it felt as if I'd been struck by lightning. He ended his communication saying, "Please have faith in my honest intentions. Love, Ken."

I carefully put the telegram and letter back in the exact same way I'd found them before I went into shock. I was heartbroken, anxious and panicked. I couldn't let Mother know I'd read the telegram and letter of course, so I had to pretend, just as she was pretending, that everything was fine. All she said to me when I asked was that my father had to go out of town for a few days—something to do with work, and I was forced to keep all my feelings locked inside.

It would be over sixty years before I found and read the other two handwritten letters my father sent from the road that summer, containing revelations that would have confused me even more at the age I was then. In his next message to Mother, my father wrote:

> I do hope you understand why I had to leave the way I did. I am not running away but simply doing something I probably should have done when I got off the band.

It becomes obvious that his crisis has at least something to do with becoming dependent on his wife financially rather than her depending on him which—although he doesn't use the word—made him feel emasculated. He talks about needing to overcome a weakness in himself that he seems helpless against. He says that he has "harbored suicidal thoughts at times" when he became "disgusted and ashamed and despondent over my lack of will power."

> This getting away from it all is not an escape, only something I had to do to find myself for myself. It would take a good psychia-

trist to figure it all out. But I must stop lying, cheating and living two lives in my mind and I can't do it when I'm home.

My dad urges his wife to think of his absence "as though I have decided to move myself and family to a different location and that naturally a husband might precede his family by a short time–as many, many men have done."

In the next paragraph, he says: "there is no point listing the lies of the recent past" before telling Mother to make a couple of phone calls in regard to band concerts he's supposed to be playing for, and say that he is out of town on an emergency. He ends the letter saying, "I am sick at heart at what I've caused . . . I will write every day and hope for the best" before ending with, "All my love, Ken."

I am greatly saddened reading this letter, written when my father was thirty-five years old. The line in which he confesses to harboring suicidal thoughts jumps out at me like a neon sign. I was a few years younger than he was when I felt that taking my life was the only way out of the guilt and shame I was feeling so deeply at that time. I'm also jolted by his words, "lies of the recent past," which make it clear that my father was not only capable of lying to his wife, but that he had been doing so for a long time. The falsehoods he is referring to seem to be about money, though perhaps there were lies about other things as well?

In his last letter, written from Salt Lake City, my dad describes how attractive he finds the layout of the town before revealing how much he dislikes living in Kansas.

> I wish you could have been here to enjoy the sights. I feel certain of one thing, Ruth, I never want to live in flat Kansas again. Of course, sometimes we must do what we don't want, but if it's possible, give me the hills & mountains & water.

The phrase "I never want to live in flat Kansas again" seems to imply that he might never return. Though my father came back less than two weeks later, it felt like an eternity to me at the time.

. . . . .

In the black-and-white snapshots from the next couple years, the

A Few (Nearly) Normal Years

three of us look like a normal, happy family. Our summer vacations took us from horseback riding in Colorado to the Carlsbad Caverns in New Mexico and, one year, all the way to California. Seat belts had yet to be invented and I had the back seat of the car to stretch out in anytime I felt like it. My father and mother often drove all night, taking turns—to save money on motels I now realize—while I slept. When they were both awake, presumably assuming that I could sleep through anything, they would often laugh while singing funny songs I'd never heard before.

The two of them driving together for long hours and singing together to help themselves stay awake must have been reminiscent of their time crisscrossing the country with the band. It clearly put them in a good mood. Their affectionate laughter and duets, combined with the rhythm of the road, made me feel happy, safe and secure.

During our visit to California, my father drove the three of us down to the place where he and Ruth Ann had met at Mission Beach in San Diego. From there, he continued driving into Mexico, which was then an easy crossing, without passports or questions. Daddy seemed especially relaxed and content on that vacation.

Back home, the little tufts of grass we'd planted when our house was new had joined together to form even, green lawns. Daddy bought a croquet set and taught me how to play. A stray yellow cat we named Butter adopted us, which pleased Mother greatly. My dad brought home a German shepherd puppy, naming him Blitz and trained him to come when he whistled a special three-note sound created just for him. He was the dog my dad had long wanted, and who would soon become my best friend.

A few months later, my aunt was driving as we rushed Mother, moaning in agony in the back seat, to the hospital emergency room where she was diagnosed with what was then referred to as a tubular pregnancy. I never discovered whether there was no chance of her getting pregnant after that or whether the doctor told her it would be too dangerous to try. I know, from a number of references in their letters to each other, that my dad and Ruth Ann had hoped and planned to have what she always referred to as "a child of their own."

Losing the dream of having her own baby with my father must have been devastating and depressing to Mother and extremely disappointing to Daddy as well. To have that desire thwarted most likely impacted their relationship and influenced their future in all sorts of subtle ways.

. . . . .

After watching several other young people about to enter their teens take the plunge at church, I dutifully went forward one Sunday morning to be immersed in baptism. As the preacher raised me up out of the water, removing the cloth he had held over my nose and mouth, I felt cleansed, purified, and newly protected by God. One reward for this rite of passage was finally getting to taste the freshly baked unleavened bread supplied by the church ladies, and picking up my own little cup for a sip of grape juice when the silver communion trays were passed down the rows of pews on Sunday morning.

An additional baptismal bonus was being welcomed into the "Young People's Class" that met before church services every Sunday evening. Becoming part of the church's teenage group included shared outings such as the monthly skating rink nights, autumn hayrides, and other special activities, which gave me a previously unexperienced feeling of inclusion and acceptance. My bonds with the young people in that community grew during the church-sponsored summer sleep-away camps I attended in Arkansas.

By the time I turned fourteen, I had experienced my first kiss and a few more. My interest in the opposite sex was quickly expanding, though nothing beyond kissing and what was then called "necking" had yet occurred. In the meantime, my parents' arguments were increasing. I was sometimes awakened in the middle of the night, by the sound of Mother's disgruntled voice growing louder by the minute. My father's more measured and subdued voice would break in occasionally. One memorable night, he grabbed a blanket and pillow, locked himself in the bathroom, and slept in the bathtub until morning. Before long, he began spending more time out of town, perhaps because his job demanded it, though it must surely have been partly to break away from his wife's constant preachy nagging.

I am struck with the awareness that once Mother bit into a subject or began trying to persuade someone of her opinion about anything, it was as if she literally could not stop talking. The person she was talking to would begin to feel badgered. She didn't seem to have the ability to consider, much less accept, a point of view that differed from her own.

Ruth Ann no longer counted on my father to mete out any punishment she deemed I deserved or needed in order for her to "teach me a lesson." If her constant criticism and belittling wasn't eliciting some kind of response from me, she would grab both of my forearms and begin vigorously trying to "shake some sense into me," to use her words. Her long fingernails digging into the backs of my arms would often break the skin. If she was particularly upset, she would slap me across the face. This stinging rebuke caused my nose to bleed a couple of times which, oddly perhaps, only served to make me feel more defiant. I always stifled my anger, never yelling back, just seething silently while my resentment against her continued to build. I was unaware that my anger, as well as the sadness that lay underneath, was being stuffed down deeper and deeper into my subconsciousness.

I acted out through subtle duplicity, secretly wearing one of my mother's blouses to school, then returning it to same spot before she got home for instance, or putting rocks in the bottom of the bucket I was supposed to be filling with dandelion weeds so that it looked as if I'd completed the task. The first time Mother discovered that I had turned the TV on while she wasn't there, you'd have thought I'd killed the cat. After that I always set a box of frozen peas on the top of the flat-topped set while watching American Bandstand. By moving the box around every few minutes and taking it off at just the right time before turning the TV off, it wouldn't be warm if Mother decided to run her hand across its top.

I recognize now that the more exasperated Mother became with my father and with her inability to bend things to her will in regard to him, the more she took out her frustration out on me. She began trying desperately to shape my behavior.

My most rebellious act, perhaps, came in the spring of my last year in junior high school. Having helped decorate the gym for the ninth grade sock hop and knowing the boy I had a crush on would be there fueled my determination to go to the dance in outright defiance of my mother who, despite my reasoned arguments and outright pleading, had remained firmly against it. The church taught that all actions and even all thoughts were either good or bad. Any kind of dancing was considered a sin. I did not understand why dancing would send me to Hell. The only explanation I'd heard had something to do with impure thoughts.

When the night for the dance arrived, I walked out of the house, then ran the few blocks to my best friend's house, zigzagging behind trees and through back yards—most were unfenced in those days—scared that Mother would show up at any moment. My friend's mother, feeling sympathy for me, quickly drove us both to the school.

> I see Mother's car pulling up to the front of the building just as we are going inside and I run quickly into the girl's bathroom. Before I can hide in one of the stalls, she comes marching in—furious—to confront me. There are a couple other girls in the restroom, which is likely what keeps her from physically grabbing me by an arm and forcibly dragging me out. After a quick hissed, clenched-jaw lecture, she tells me in no uncertain terms to come to the car, turns abruptly, and leaves, clearly expecting me to follow her. I ignore her completely, turn the other way, and rush toward the gym and the sound of the Everly Brothers singing "Wake Up Little Susie." As soon as it becomes clear that Mother has thought better of coming into a large room full of students and teachers and making a scene, I relax and enjoy myself.

Exhilarated when I managed to master the jitterbug that night, I had no impure thoughts. A bunch of ninth-graders and some of their teachers were having fun; what was bad or sinful about that? The freedom to move my body in time to music seemed liberating in some fundamental way. It would be over two years, however, before I would attend another dance and by that time I was living in a different city, with a new stepmother.

All these years later, I experience a surge of compassion for Mother. I can envisage how utterly unhappy and defeated she must have been feeling that night as she began to recognize she couldn't even control me, let alone my father, any longer.

Did she leave the door unlocked on purpose and shut herself in her bedroom so she wouldn't have to see me when I came home that night? Was she angry or depressed or both because my father wasn't there? Did she ever tell him what I had done?

So many things could have gone wrong the night I crawled out my bedroom window, after putting pillows and clothes under the covers to make it look as if I was still there. My neighbor friend did the same and met me in the middle of the deserted street at midnight. As she had arranged, a car drove up and we quickly hopped into it with a couple of boys she knew who may or may not have been old enough to drive, and who may or may not have been drunk. They seemed more interested in boasting and showing off than in any hands-on interaction with us. As I remember it, they just drove, way faster than they should have been, around the streets in our neighborhood for a while before finally stopping back at the spot where they'd picked us up before they quickly sped away, guffawing loudly.

. . . . .

A few months later, my father drove me to church to drop me off for the Young People's Meeting before the Sunday evening service. We were early, which I imagine he had planned. After parking the car, Daddy turned to me and said he had something he wanted to tell me. He then stated calmly that he was leaving Ruth Ann. He confided that he was seeing someone else, adding quite matter-of-factly that they were not engaged in a sexual relationship but that he cared very much for her. I wasn't shocked. I couldn't blame him for choosing not be with Mother, or for wanting to be with someone else. In that moment, I was actually happy for him.

When he mentioned that he was going to be moving to another town, a couple of hours away, that took me a minute to digest. As I begged him to take me with him, he patiently explained why that wouldn't work, since he was basically a traveling salesman and he couldn't leave me alone for days at a time. I was devastated, and adamant that I did not want to live alone with Mother. I even told Daddy about the shaking and face slapping, and showed him the scars on the backs of my forearms.

My father likely anticipated my reaction as he clearly had an ace up his sleeve. He offered me a solution I was okay with—enrolling me in an academy for high school students situated on the campus of a Christian college in Arkansas. Having met a couple of kids at the summer church camp who had spoken about this high school and, seeing it as an escape from the palpable distress and uncertainty surrounding me, I was eager to go. The hardest thing was leaving our dog, Blitz, and I was heartbroken a couple months later when I was told he had bitten someone and had to be put down.

Was that story actually true? Mother never wanted a dog or bonded with Blitz. In fact she put that ad in the paper to give him away after he dug up her petunias and I called and cancelled it, pretending to be her. Is it possible that with both my father and me gone she just didn't want to take care of a dog she never really liked, or want him around? Could Blitz, in his misery, have suddenly become aggressive? How would he have gotten out of the fenced back yard?

Chapter Seven

The Phone Call, the Meeting, and a Visitation

I believe not only that trauma is curable but that the healing process can be a catalyst for profound awakening.

—Peter A. Levine

Life will give us whatever experience is most helpful for the evolution of our consciousness.

—Eckhart Tolle

I am living with my father, his current wife, and her two young daughters. My newest stepmother is pregnant. I am a few weeks away from boarding a train to travel to a town I've never been to and a place I've never seen to begin my first year of college. I happen to be near the telephone when it rings and pick up the receiver.

"Hello."

"Is this Dawn?"

"Yes."

"Dawn, this is your mother."

My stepmother, watching from the kitchen a few feet away, would later say she saw my face turn white as I sank into the small chair next to the phone and she knew I was in shock. I remember nothing else of the telephone conversation although, clearly, the low-voiced woman on the other end of the phone line said something about wanting to meet me, and I presumably expressed a similar interest. She mentioned driving to Kansas City, saying she would be bringing her son.

Around the time of my seventeenth birthday, a few weeks before the startling phone call, I had asked my father, "Do you think my mother ever thinks about me? Do I look anything like her?" I'm uncertain what effect my questions had on my father or even how he answered them. However, unbeknownst to me, after my query he had looked into his first wife's current whereabouts, explicitly stating in his inquiry—he told me after her phone call—that she was not to contact me in any way.

A few weeks later, my father drove me to the motel where Penny had checked in with her twelve-year-old son. I have no recollection as to why I decided to "dress up" for this meeting, or what words might have been exchanged between me and my dad during that drive.

When we entered the motel room, I encountered a slim, dark-haired woman, slightly shorter than I was. She had brown eyes like mine. I couldn't help but notice the similarities in our facial structure. We were both wearing brown sheath-style dresses and the same color and style high-heeled shoes. I remember thinking, in those first few awkward seconds when time seemed to stand still, "I am in the presence of both my parents for the first time in my life that I am conscious of."

What must it have been like for Daddy seeing Penny again? Was he able to detach from whatever emotions he must surely have been experiencing and just remain cordial and calm the way he often seemed to? Or was he just repressing what he was actually feeling?

My father and I were introduced to the thin, blond-haired boy in the room. My half-brother seemed somewhat timid, or perhaps it was apprehension I sensed in him. My father soon excused himself and left for a while. I think he may have told me beforehand that he was going to do that. Looking back on it, I'm sure he felt my nervousness, and was trying to protect me from too much emotional overload. He might have also been protecting himself. I'm guessing he had a cup of coffee and a cigarette in some nearby cafe. I do not recall how long I stayed in the hotel room that first day or what conversations may have ensued. I'm fairly certain that I was, at least partially, emotionally "numbed out."

I remember going with my newfound mother and brother to a local swimming pool the next day, with my current boyfriend in tow, and attending an AA meeting that evening. Penny must surely have mentioned how many years she'd been sober and why she didn't want to miss

The Phone Call, the Meeting, and a Visitation

an Alcoholics Anonymous meeting. I had some vague understanding that her drinking had played a part in her abandonment of me; however, I had zero experience with alcohol and was completely ignorant about alcohol addiction. The recitations, declarations, and confessions during the gathering, which included close to a couple dozen men and woman of varying ages sitting on foldout chairs, reminded me a bit of going to church, with caffeinated coffee and glazed donuts substituting for Sunday communion.

. . . . .

A few months later, during my December break from college classes, I felt both excited and nervous as I stepped onto a commercial airplane for the first time in my life, and flew to Florida to visit my birth mother and my half-brother in their suburban home in Miami. I presume Penny instigated the visit and possibly paid for the plane ticket. Meeting Penny's then wheelchair-bound mother, who was living with her daughter and grandson, I had the impression that she was a woman who once had a large personality and a commanding presence but now found herself diminished and resented it deeply. Seemingly completely uninterested in any interaction with me, she mostly confined herself to her room in the house during my visit.

Penny invited several people into her home for the purpose of meeting me: a best friend from AA; a couple of neighbors; and a man wearing a clerical collar whom she was clearly very fond of, and possibly wanting to impress. They all seemed extremely happy to meet me. I felt as if I was being put on display like a new doll or toy.

Did Penny think we were just going to go forward as a loving mother and daughter who found each other after nearly twenty years, as if our separation had nothing to do with her? Maybe someone told her that her daughter was looking for her and wanted to meet her? Is it possible she had prayed for this miracle which then seemed to be happening?

On my last night there, Penny drove her son and me to the Boca Raton Country Club for dinner so she could introduce me to her brother who she told me, with obvious pride, was the manager there. I suspect he was the head waiter in the dining room. He didn't actually take a seat and eat with us but stopped by the table and sat for a short time. I remember him as handsome and extremely cordial. Penny clearly adored him. It seemed as if Penny and I both had a desire at that point to forge a relationship with one another although I can't remember much, if any, authentic conversations of depth during that visit.

I was a bit surprised when Penny decided to come to my wedding in 1963. I had two other mothers already in town for the occasion, although my father's current wife was, of course, the official mother of the bride that day. Weddings were much simpler events back then, at least in a small college town in Nebraska. As it turned out—each mother thinking another was helping me I suppose—I got into my wedding dress by myself in my dorm room and carefully walked the two blocks to the church building. Penny happened to show up in the church basement just as our volunteer photographer was about to take a picture of me. She introduced herself to him as my mother and, perhaps seeing the resemblance, he quickly posed her behind me as if she was helping me with my dress.

Six months later, my new husband gave up a few days of study time during a break in his classes to drive us from the town in Texas where we were living to a very nice mobile home park in Florida where my retired fraternal grandparents lived. They had been unable to come to our wedding and were eager to meet their new grandson-in-law. It was always a great joy for me to spend time with my grandparents who had been the most consistently stabilizing influence in my life up to that point. After a sweet but short stay with them, we drove to where Penny and my half-brother were living, for an even shorter visit, before driving back to Texas.

During the next few years, Penny and I exchanged newsy letters occasionally. I signed mine "Love, Dawn." She signed hers, " Love always, Always Love" and at the bottom of one, "Your Loving Mother." When our first child was born, I believe my husband must have called her to let her know. She sent a telegram saying, "So glad your ordeal is over," and mailed a package containing three hand-knit (presumably by her) wool soakers which were meant to be worn over a baby's diaper. They were pretty and unusual although, naive as I was at the time, they seemed so impractical that I never used them. They remain, to this day, neatly ar-

The Phone Call, the Meeting, and a Visitation

ranged in the square, white box they arrived in.

. . . . .

By 1974, my husband and I, sadly, had separated, and I had returned with our two children, to Northern California to attend graduate school. Penny's mother had died and she and I had fallen somewhat out of touch. While our children were with their father that summer, I caught a ride to the central east coast with friends and then arranged a short flight to Florida to see Penny and the man she had been living with for a number of years.

When they picked me up at the airport, one of the first things Penny said was, "You don't mind if we make a quick stop to have a drink, do you?" The sudden realization that a confirmed alcoholic was no longer sober, was a bolt from the blue and disconcerting to say the least. Caught by surprise, I began to feel anxious, and somewhat trapped in a situation I didn't have a clue how to handle. I went into mental autopilot mode while hiding my feelings inside a facade of equanimity.

As we reached the area where Penny and her partner lived, I noted that their trailer home seemed somewhat remote, with only a few other mobile homes surrounded by large parcels of land. The three of us ate dinner together in the rather cramped space. I believe wine appeared with the meal. I remained smiling and polite. Blaming my tiredness on jet lag, although I had not, in fact, come from a different time zone, I went to bed in their small guest bedroom as early as I could manage.

Awakened an hour or so later by a heated argument which seemed to be getting physical, between two apparently intoxicated people, I overheard Penny say accusingly, "Are you saying my daughter is better than my son!" and her companion answering "No, I just said she seems like a nice girl." The voices became muffled for a few moments, and then I distinctly heard the word "gun." Unnerved, I quickly dressed and slipped out of the side door of the trailer. Seeing a light on in the adjacent mobile home, I took refuge with the understanding young couple who answered my knock. When I explained why I was there, they told me that their neighbors were both "really nice people, except when they get drunk," before confirming that they did indeed own a gun which had been shot at least once that they were aware of. They invited me stay the rest of the night with them, ushering me to a cushioned platform bed in the back of the trailer where I could look out the window and keep watch on the one I'd escaped from. I slept very little.

There was no way to avoid returning to Penny and her mate's trailer the next morning. I knocked gently and someone said, "Come in." I immediately noticed that Penny had bruises forming around one eye and that her companion had several deep scratches on one side of his face. We sat in mostly awkward silence waiting for my half-brother, who was driving from another part of the state, with his young family, in order to see me. The obvious "elephant in the room" loomed large but was never addressed.

My brother arrived, later than expected, which seemed to annoy his mother. His wife appeared shy and slightly uncomfortable or maybe just very tired. She had a cute baby in her arms and a sweet little girl who looked to be around four years old. I'm not certain how I acquired a few snapshots I have from that day. In the one of me with Penny, neither of us is smiling. I look stunned, taciturn, and like I might be sick at any moment. She looks resigned or possibly a bit defiant. Our physical resemblance, however, is unmistakable.

The neighbors who had offered me solace the night before offered to drive me to the airport, and no one objected. I remained dazed for a good while. I have no memory whatsoever of getting on the airplane or disembarking wherever it landed.

. . . . .

In late December of 1976, I flew from California to Kansas City and my father arranged to drive himself and me to Florida to see Penny in the hospital where she was dying of lung cancer. He and I talked about

The Phone Call, the Meeting, and a Visitation

all kinds of things during that drive, except the fact that the first woman he had loved and married, and who had given birth to me, was nearing death. And of course we had no clue that he himself would die from the same disease only thirteen years later.

Seeing Penny emaciated and tinged with death at the age of fifty-six was disquieting and it elicited a wave of compassion in me. The oxygen tent canopied over the top half of her bed meant that she had to lift up the side and stick her head out to speak. She asked for some caviar shortly after we arrived, which her son dutifully went off to try to locate for her, and my father likely went off in search of coffee. Finding myself alone in the room with Penny for a brief period, and cognizant of the fact that I wouldn't have the chance again, I asked her if she remembered anything in particular about my birth. I recorded her response in a journal I was keeping at the time:

> I was knocked out for the last 5 or 6 hours and I didn't see you until you were 6 hours old. I don't think that's a good way to give birth. I think it takes away from the love a mother should feel for her child.

Years later, a friend pointed out that Penny seemed to be blaming the medical facility or her doctor for her failure to bond with me. However, her words seemed like the only apology I was ever going to get and I took them as such. She gave birth to her son five years after I was born, presumably under different and much better circumstances, and it would seem that she bonded with him from the beginning.

When Penny's physician appeared, and I introduced myself to him in the hallway, he said to me, "What does she have against you?" Taken aback, and wondering what had provoked his question, I responded with the only answer that came to me. "Her own guilt I guess," I replied, mentioning that she had abandoned me when I was a year old. He said nothing more, and I didn't see him again. I recall little else about that somewhat surreal time except that saying goodbye, knowing this was the last time I would ever see the woman who had helped give me life, produced a flood of emotion from some deep, primordial place in me.

A few weeks later, during the night or very early morning, of January 10, 1977, something occurred that was vividly visual, palpable, and galvanizing.

> **Penny appears at the foot of my bed. She is wearing a long white garment made of gauzy material. It looks like something between a wedding dress and a nightgown. Her countenance is distraught. She looks confused and somewhat angry. I sit straight up in my bed, looking directly at her. I am captivated by her presence and by her appearance so close and clear. Both her arms are stretched out in front of her as if to show me the double row of heavy-looking iron chains hanging from her wrists. I feel sad for her. I feel tears wetting my face as I spontaneously say out loud, "I forgive you." I repeat it several times, "I forgive you. I forgive you." I see the chains loosen, and drop slowly, soundlessly to the floor. Her face begins to soften slightly as her image slowly fades from my view.**

I was grateful for the encounter, and for the fact that Penny had been able to contact me as she transitioned out of her body. Her shackled appearance made me realize what a heavy burden of guilt she must have been carrying her entire life regarding her failure, or her inability, to give me the care I needed and deserved as an infant. Something seemed to shift for me as I kept assuring her that I forgave her. I thought at the time, naively perhaps, that this interaction had settled the matter of her abandonment of me. In fact, it would be a good many years before that resolution would occur.

A few hours later, Penny's son called to tell me his mother had died, which of course I already knew. I didn't tell him about her "visitation," though I made some reference about a feeling I had in regard to her having left her body. After a moment of silence between us, I commented that she'd had a pretty hard life to which he quickly replied, "Well, she held it together long enough to raise me." We communicated a few times shortly after that. However, both of us were in the midst of busy lives, raising children, and living on separate coasts. We eventually lost touch, and have never seen each other again nor has he responded to my efforts to contact him.

If I had been more conscious, more open, more in touch with long-buried feelings I had yet to uncover, maybe my birth mother and I could have had more meaningful conversations. What if she had ever asked me to forgive her? What if I'd been able find my voice and been able to tell her how alarmed and sad I felt about her losing her sobriety instead of judging her? Maybe if I'd been mature enough, if I'd been able to feel more compassion for her sooner, perhaps she and I might have forged a deeper relationship.

In the midst of these flitting thoughts, I recognize the utter futility of my "if only" thinking. I remind myself that the inability to accept the way things are, or the way things were, is how suffering occurs. We cannot change or re-create the past. "It was what it was" must surely be as applicable a mantra as the idiomatic phrase now printed on everything from T-shirts to coffee mugs, "It is what it is." If either my birth mother or I had been able to make different decisions during our lives at the time we made them, we would have. We all make the choices we do given our level of ability and conscious awareness at any given point in our lives.

Chapter Eight

Ramifications and Reverberations

The consequences of trauma can be widespread and hidden symptoms can remain dormant, accumulating over years or even decades.
—Peter A. Levine

I didn't realize how attached I was to having somebody else confirm me as being OK... In other words, it didn't come from inside me. It came from someone else's view of me.
—Pema Chödrön

"Have you ever been raped?"

"Well, no," I replied slowly, "not really, though I have had nonconsensual sex a few times."

"Dawn, nonconsensual sex is rape!"

"Well, I never had a gun to my head or a knife to my throat." The loved one who had asked me the question seemed astounded and repeated the words with greater emphasis, "Nonconsensual sex is rape!"

Many years ago, a friend said to me, "Oh Dawn you give up your power so easily." I didn't really understand what she meant at the time. Looking back on it, I recognize now how my decision to simply detach from my body/mind and endure unwanted sexual encounters was connected to imprinting from my early childhood. I had let my self-worth be determined by other people's opinions and attitudes. In my need to be "good," to not upset anyone, to be loved and accepted, I became reluctant to ever say no. Layered over that were words from a hymn I had sung hundreds of times in my younger years which had taken root in my subconscious. "Angry words oh let them never from my tongue unbridled slip. May the heart's best impulse ever, check them ere they soil the lip." I came to accept that it was a moral sin to even feel angry, let alone give voice to such thoughts or energy; and I suppressed any impulse to do so for many years.

When I began examining the details of my first year of life, as well as reflecting on the unpredictability, insecurity, and emotional abuse that occurred intermittently during the next few years, I became increasingly aware of fixed ideas, habits of mind and persistent behaviors that seemed to stem from the seminal trauma I was exploring.

Surely there was something wrong with me if the woman who gave birth to me didn't love me enough to take care of me and then deserted me. I must have been flawed, bad, wrong, undeserving of love. I didn't just drive away my first mother but another mother and, initially at least, the next mother. "I'm not good enough" became a deeply engrained belief that shaped my personality and influenced my choices and conduct for years to come. I was constantly judging myself, trying to fix myself, edit myself, continually adapting my behavior in an effort to please others in order to gain their approval so they would love me.

Very early in life, I developed the ability to "read" people. I could sense their moods, along with their emotional and mental states. This allowed me to adjust my actions to what the adults in control wanted from me. I became adept at deciphering the rules and following them, at deducing how people wanted me to behave so that I could act accordingly in order to please them and to avoid conflict or consequences. This skill helped me maintain the image of being a "good little girl." For much of my childhood and young adulthood I was basically trying my best to be good enough, compliant enough, pretty enough, polite enough, quiet enough, useful enough so that I would not be rejected or abandoned.

Discovering the art of drama and performing on stage by the time I reached high school had given me a boost in self-confidence. The mask of acting became an acceptable and energizing form of being seen and heard. Inhabiting the personality and mannerisms of fictional or historic characters let me "come out" in disguise, giving me a safe place to shine, earning me recognition and awards in the process. Acting aided me in

beginning to rise above (or possibly bury more deeply in my unconscious) my low self-esteem issues and fear of rejection. It allowed me to present a polished persona to the world, while parts of my essential self remained unseen and unclaimed. This cloaking device served me well through my school years and beyond, including a summer playing Portia at a large outdoor theater, six months of travel with the Shakespeare company, and into the professional acting world in the California Bay Area during the 1970's and early 1980's.

. . . . .

He was nineteen; I was eighteen when I fell in love with my first husband, a good looking, soft-spoken, straight-A student in the two-year college we were both attending on full scholarships (mine in theater and his academic). He was highly respected by teachers and students alike. I thought he was the closest thing to a saint I'd ever met. I think some part of me reasoned that if I was with him, my life would be perfect and that some of those saintly qualities would rub off on me. In reality, we were both naïve and inexperienced young people who came from completely different worlds and who barely knew each other when we married a year later. Our personalities had been formed from such divergent backgrounds and environments that, although we felt drawn to each other, and had declared our love and loyalty, it eventually became increasingly difficult to find common ground in terms of our individual needs and aspirations.

My new husband was like my father in some ways—intelligent, kind, stoical. Yet, as I would discover, he too was often physically and emotionally absent. Our histories differed radically. His parents had met on the Wind River Indian Reservation in Wyoming—home to Eastern Shoshone and Northern Arapaho tribes—where his mother had been hired as a cook and his father as a mechanic. They began their life together in a two-room log cabin on a remote piece of land known as Owl

Creek. Their first several children, including my husband, were born in that dirt-floored cabin before they moved into small house in a nearby town that covered two square miles and had reached its highest population of not quite 4,000 people in 1960. My mother-in-law had birthed a dozen children, three of whom died in childbirth or shortly thereafter, in a span of twenty years. In my eyes she was a true pioneer woman. I was in awe of her resilience, strength and skills. My father-in-law was a hard worker and a man of very few words. I, on the other hand, had spent the bulk of my growing up years in the largest city in Kansas, with a population of over 250,000, an only child living in a three-bedroom house with an unpredictable stepmother who worked full time at various sales and secretarial jobs. When she was home, she seemed to never stop talking.

My husband and I moved to West Texas a few months before the historically shocking event of President Kennedy's assassination, November 22, 1963, so that he could finish his double-major undergraduate degree at a four-year Christian college there. We stayed three more years so that he could complete a Bachelor of Divinity degree which he accomplished while working part-time at jobs ranging from preaching in a tiny, unincorporated cotton-farming community 100 miles away two Sundays a month to working as a gas station attendant.

One of the fringe benefits of the job I procured as Executive Secretary to the Admissions and Placement Director of the college, was free tuition for two classes each semester. This led to my making a few friends in the Theater Department and appearing in several productions. When I became pregnant, we were surprised and a bit anxious yet happy. Learning that my job would be terminated as soon as I needed to wear maternity clothes—an unfortunate discrimination that wouldn't become illegal until more than a decade later—was a shock on several levels, particularly financially. My husband took on yet another part-time job to try to make ends meet. A forward-thinking female professor I'd taken a class with, who heard about me losing my job, offered to pay me a very generous hourly fee to help her at her house. The work turned out to be several days of mostly polishing all the silver she and her husband owned. There seemed to be little else I could do to earn money at the time.

The day I went into labor, in an effort to distract and comfort myself, I got out the Scrabble board my father and I had played on so many times, with his familiar handwriting on the score pad. I hadn't played the game in a good while since my husband had neither the time nor the inclination for that particular type of diversion. The unfolded board just fit on the two-person table in the tiny kitchen area of the one-room single garage apartment we were living in. By sitting down on one side of the table, taking a turn, then switching to the other chair and taking a turn, all the while tracking the time between my contractions, I succeeded in getting through most of the day before needing to call the gas station where my husband was working to tell him I thought we should go to the hospital. Once there, he was required to sit in the waiting room reserved for expectant fathers until a nurse came out a few hours later to inform him that his daughter had been born.

Lying on my back under an incredibly bright light, legs spread-eagle, my feet in steel stirrups and experiencing particularly intense pain, something I was never told might or would occur happened. A mask came down over my face and a voice told me to count backwards from five. I only got to three. The next thing I knew, I was in a hospital bed with a nurse tapping me briskly on one cheek, saying, "Wake up, wake up! Don't you want to see your baby?" Another nurse appeared and placed a swaddled, puffy-cheeked infant with a shock of black hair in my arms. I barely had time for my mind to register that this was the baby I had given birth to before the nurse removed her from my arms and whisked her out of the room. Watching the other nurse leave the room with a bloody sheet and, realizing it must be my blood, I wondered why I was bleeding.

After two days of mostly sleeping, I was told I could get dressed to go home. A few minutes later, the nurse brought my bundled baby into the room, deposited her on the bed saying I could dress her and, without further words, quickly exited. Completely alone with this miraculous, fragile being who was now totally dependent on me, I was petrified. Although I'd done some "baby sitting" during my high school years, I had never attempted to dress a real baby or even a small child in my life.

A month or so later, sitting on a porch chair on a hot, dry summer day as evening approached, I was nursing my daughter while her father studied in the college library. As I gazed down at her face, marveling at the profound physical intimacy of feeding this tiny human being who had emerged from my body, she opened her eyes and peered into mine. Not quite letting go of my nipple completely, her little lips widened into a half smile. I knew in that instant that I would do my best to be the mother she deserved; I knew I would lay down my life for her.

. . . . .

After graduating in 1970, with his straight-A grade average still intact, my husband was soon offered ministerial jobs in three different locations in California. He chose the one in a university town in the greater Bay Area.

My husband excelled at his job and was deeply respected by everyone in the congregation of less than a hundred members. Early each morning, he walked from the three-bedroom ranch-style house we were given to live in, across an open field to his office in the church building, usually returning around dinner time. He took short breaks during the day at the basketball hoop that had been installed at one edge of the church parking lot, sometimes joking that the basketball hoop was real reason he had said yes to that particular job offer. As soon as our daughter was old enough to walk across the field by herself, with me watching from one side and her dad from the other, nothing excited her more than carrying a bag lunch over to share with him. In the meantime, I acted the part of minister's wife well, teaching Sunday School weekly, and Vacation Bible School in the summers, serving as the church secretary, creating a newsletter, and cooking dinner for different church members regularly.

Our son's drug-free birth in California was radically different in nearly every way from giving birth four years earlier in Texas. My husband took notes during the Lamaze classes we attended together, accompanied me to most of my doctor's appointments and was with me from the beginning of my labor through our son's birth. He was there for me in a time when I desperately needed not to be alone and, for me, it was a pinnacle of intimacy in our relationship. Our new baby's almost four-year-old sister became his fierce protector from the beginning, convinced she was his backup Mom, never once displaying any jealousy or feelings of being displaced.

My husband and I were bound together by the vows we had taken and by our deep love for our children. Yet I was growing increasingly lonely in the marriage, craving a kind of emotional contact he didn't know how to offer and didn't seem to need himself. Spending time with his children clearly brought him joy, though he always appeared to be happiest when he was in the library or by himself studying.

. . . . .

When one of the friends I had made through the Drama Department in Texas came to California looking for a place to stay, my husband immediately invited him to use our spare bedroom. Our guest often led singing during church services, our children liked him, and I was thrilled to have a familiar friend to talk with about things we had in common. During that time, my husband was spending one night a week out of town in order to sit in on a class with a favorite scholar/author of his at the Graduate Theological Union in Berkeley.

The guilt I experienced after letting a comforting hug with a good friend—a virginal and still-closeted gay man—lead to sex one night when my husband was away and my children sleeping, precipitated a soul-searing depression. My only thought was that I had failed utterly at being a good wife—much less a minister's wife—having now committed the grave sin of adultery. My feelings of remorse and shame seemed more than I could bear.

> **I am standing in front of the medicine cabinet, holding a new razor blade I've taken out of a container. I wonder if I have to cut both my wrists. How do I do that? I have the thought that it will be too bloody. It will make too big mess to clean up. I find a container of a prescription medication for pain. I fill the small cup by the sink with water and set it back down. I remove the cap from the container, and pour a few of the small white pills into my left hand. I set the container down on the edge of the sink. I throw the pills into my mouth, pick up the water and swallow all the tablets in one big gulp. I reach for the container to pour more pills into my hand but somehow knock it over. The pills spill out into the sink and onto the floor. The sound is enough to push a speck of light into the darkness—I cannot do this to my children . . .**

I possess a hazy memory of my husband coming home with a young couple we had recently become acquainted with after they came to a church service. She must have taken our children with her while her husband stayed at our house.

> **I feel myself being held upright. All I want to do is go to sleep. I can't seem to talk or walk. They are telling me that I have to keep walking. They tell me if I can't stay awake, then they have to take me to the hospital.**

Later, lying on the twin bed in the guest room, weeping silently, utterly bereft, I began trying to pray. There was no connection, as if a telephone line had been severed. There was simply nobody there. As my tears continued, I had an inkling that the God of my childhood beliefs did not exist.

Not long after that, my husband arranged for us to move out of the minister's house into an apartment complex in town with a swimming pool, which we all enjoyed. I made friends who weren't church members and there were children nearby for ours to play with, something they had not had up to that point. My husband and I spent a little more time together, doing things that were very new for us, such as going to a movie once or twice. The one thing we never did was share our feelings, nor did we get the help we so clearly needed.

In hindsight, I think my husband then turned to the area of life that was most familiar, satisfying and comfortable for him—academic study. He decided to go back to school to work toward a doctorate degree. After being accepted and offered financial assistance at several prestigious graduate schools on both coasts, he chose UCLA.

In my mind I was assuming we would all go together, wherever his decision took us. I do not remember what discussion we had that led us to try a trial separation at that point. I moved into a small, low-rent apartment in the town where we'd been living and, by some miracle, received a scholarship to enroll in an MFA program in theater at the university there. He took our five-year-old daughter with him to Southern California.

How did we even come to such a decision? Did I just go along with his suggestion because I thought it was what he wanted? Did he think I would be happier? How did we imagine it could possibly work to separate our family in that way, and for the two of us to go to graduate school at the same time?

Clearly, we were both unhappy, both feeling guilty, unable to communicate, flailing in the dark, and still terribly naive.

Less than a month later, I couldn't bear being away from my daughter, or the thought that she would feel I had abandoned her, nor did it feel right to keep my son separated from his father and sister. I repacked everything I'd just finished arranging, and drove to LA in an effort to reunite our family. My husband had been able to procure a space in the married students' apartments available at that time—old barracks made into duplexes inside a large fenced area along Sepulveda Boulevard—although it seemed as if he was seldom there. He studied in the library on campus after his classes and often came home after the children and I were asleep.

At some point we made a decision to participate in an experimental shared living situation with a couple residing in the apartment just across from us—cooking meals together, trading child care and so on. Although I enjoyed having an enthusiastic cooking partner and female friend, the trial was fairly short-lived and did little if anything to improve my primary adult relationship.

Securing an appointment for us at the UCLA counseling center gave me hope that professional advice might offer us a way forward. Near the end of our session, the therapist said he really couldn't help us, adding that we were like two people standing at either end of a swimming pool and neither of us was willing to jump in. My husband moved out physically a short time later, into a house with a few other grad students within walking distance from the university so that I would have a car.

Finding myself essentially a single mom with two young children and very little money, I sometimes sold my government-issued food stamps in order to pay for other necessities, such as the special shoes I was told my son needed to have to prevent his feet from pronating. Having heard from someone that grocery stores were forced to discard good food that hasn't been sold, I tried "dumpster diving" late at night while my children were asleep in the car. Though I did find things like potatoes and carrots that were still perfectly fine for cooking and eating, the surreptitious nature of the endeavor and the feeling that I was doing something illegal prevented me from continuing that particular practice for very long.

At the end of that summer, I went back to Northern California with both children. I was able to secure subsidized housing for us, and we all three began school that fall: nursery, elementary, and graduate. Still holding onto the thought that my husband and I would somehow find a way to evolve our relationship and that our family would be reunited, I couldn't bring myself to think about divorce. He finally initiated the process nearly two years later. We had no assets and had already divided our belongings so the procedure was simple. In spite of the fact that it clearly needed to be done, and we had both moved on to other relationships, signing the divorce papers was heart-wrenching. We still loved each other. He sent me what little money he could each month and our children spent summers with him, as well as long weekends when they became old enough to fly alone.

. . . . .

While working toward my Master of Fine Arts degree, teaching an undergraduate acting class and dramatizing patient roles for third-year medical students to help pay my rent and other bills, I met the man who would eventually become my second husband when we were cast opposite each other in a theatrical production.

After my first marriage ended, I was reluctant to commit to monogamy in a sexual relationship again. Having broken my marriage vows and still feeling guilty about it, I thought it better to avoid such a promise. I had difficulty trusting others, especially anyone I began a romantic relationship with, not to leave me; I hadn't yet realized that I needed to be able to love myself instead of depending on someone else to generate my self-worth. Because I had no confidence that any good relationship would last and an underlying fear of future abandonment, I now see that, subconsciously, I needed to have someone in the wings, a spare relationship so to speak. Layered into my reluctance to commit to a monogamous relationship was the fact that I had never had the chance to explore my own sexuality before I married. Giving myself permission to do that led to some surreptitious and ill-advised decisions on my part, yet it also helped me reach a point of being able to freely choose and commit to monogamy eventually.

Over time, I began to notice how deeply habituated I was to continually adapting and going along with what others seemed to want, how I always let the other person in a relationship define situations and make decisions for me in order to avoid their potential upset, displeasure or rejection. I became aware of how often I felt frustrated, irritated, or resentful underneath my show of acquiescence. To this day, I still feel myself slipping into a "tuning out" and disconnecting response when I feel judged or made wrong. I sometimes mistake someone's impassioned opinion about a matter as disparagement or as critical response to something I've said or done. I am now able to recognize when that is happening and consciously change my response most of the time, yet the habit is deeply ingrained.

My Jewish husband, the product of a dialectical culture that thrives on passionate discourse, was raised to express his feelings fully and completely as they surfaced, including what might be called healthy anger. It was a trait I was so unaccustomed to that, while some small part of me almost admired this ability, I felt easily overpowered by the intensity of his efforts to engage me in this particular way. Early in our relationship, long before we married, he encouraged, even pushed me, to express my thoughts and feelings, whatever they were. Years later he confessed to sometimes starting arguments with me in order to "draw out your energy." What he perceived as healthy exchanges, I took as escalating criticism and conflict; and I experienced the energy being directed at me as physically and emotionally overwhelming. When this occurred, I would retreat, simply disappear for hours, or even days sometimes or, occasionally, declare that the relationship was over.

There came a day when my husband and I were quarreling and I became so angry that I took a seldom-used tube of red lipstick to write a message to him on the wall-to-wall mirror in our bathroom. I wrote some pretty horrible things, using several swear words I had never uttered aloud, before grabbing my car keys, slamming the front door behind me as hard as I could and driving to a movie theater. I have no clue what film I was watching when halfway through the movie, I went into great angst, ruminating about what I'd done, I felt I had probably ruined my relationship with my husband, and that he would surely never forgive me.

Daring to hope there was some chance he hadn't yet seen the missive on the mirror, I left the theater and drove home. Creeping slowly in through the front door, feeling small, childish, and dejected, with tears in my eyes, I was stunned when my husband greeted me with open arms. He then grabbed me gently by my shoulders, looked me in the eye and said enthusiastically, "Dawn, do you recognize that this is the first time you've gotten in touch with your anger in the moment you were feeling it, and were able to express that!"

I gradually became more comfortable communicating my own point of view without feeling guilty or ashamed. My husband and I began using communication skills that supported us in having productive discussions instead of arguments when disagreements arise, and I learned to set limits on the amount of time I am able to engage in such exchanges. We came up with a strategy many years ago that has proven practical and beneficial. When a conflict between us begins to escalate and we feel ourselves becoming more deeply entrenched in our personal positions on some matter, either of us can retrieve a tattered white "flag" on a stick which we keep in a special place, and wave it in the air. This action does not mean the person waving it surrenders to the other's position. It is simply a reminder that we have agreed to never make a personal point of view or preference more important than our commitment to our relationship.

. . . . .

According to the International Society for Traumatic Stress Studies and other sources, the effects of childhood trauma can impact an adult's life emotionally, mentally and physically in a number of ways. Paradoxically perhaps, all trauma also provides an opportunity for growth and transformation. I still struggle now and then to identify and articulate my authentic feelings. I occasionally experience short bouts of depression or sadness when I feel misunderstood, judged, criticized, or unheard. I notice myself caught between feeling angry about not being seen and trying to hide myself. My brain still reacts when I am told I *should* do something, and I continue to find escalating volume in spirited discussions that sometimes turn into arguments energetically draining. However, I am now usually able to express what I am feeling when I am feeling it. I no longer *believe* everything I think or identify with every emotion that arises.

I have come to recognize, and focus on, the positive things that have come to me in life in spite of—or possibly even because of—the toxic stress and trauma I experienced in my infancy and early childhood. I have learned not only that demons can turn out to be angels in disguise but that what seems like adversity can turn into grace.

Chapter Nine

Portals to Awakening

Who Am I?

Disconnection from the Self is the first thing that happens in trauma . . . the greatest calamity wasn't that there was no longer support, but that you lost connection to your Essence.

—Gabor Maté

A perception, sudden as blinking, that subject and object are one, will lead to a deeply mysterious, wordless understanding: and by this understanding you will awaken to the truth.

—Hung Po

In 1978, a longtime friend told me about a residential meditation retreat she had recently attended. She said it was the most powerful practice she'd ever experienced. She also mentioned that while she was participating in this three-day intensive retreat, she reached a place where she faced death. That sounded a bit scary, so I didn't think much more about it as I continued my massage school certification training and exploring various therapeutic, somatic and yogic practices.

A couple of years later, I ended up participating in the type of retreat my friend had mentioned. I found the dyad, or partner assisted meditation, a refreshing and energizing format. It seemed superior to meditating alone, reciting a mantra, or focusing my attention on an object or even solely on my breath. Sitting opposite another individual, receiving an instruction such as, "Tell me who you are," and then being listened to attentively, without interruption, or comment beyond, "Thank you," before the partner's roles reversed was, in and of itself, an extremely useful and beneficial exercise.

I was impressed by the fact that the process being taught empowered the individual, rather than the leader. I was relieved that it didn't seem to be connected to any particular religion or belief system, and that participants were not asked to join a center, a sect, or a movement at the end of the three days.

At the time, though I didn't fully understand the subtleties of the technique we were using, I did notice that when I put my attention on myself and contemplated who I was, my communications slowly grew simpler and more concise. I also observed that I had some deep attachments to certain ways of thinking about myself. Close to the end of the three days, I became aware that I was the one asking: "Who am I?"

My main takeaway was power of the primary activity, basically combining an age-old Rinzai Zen koan practice with a modern communication process. I was affected by the depth of the contact that grew as the forty-minute dyads with different partners continued, by the way the practice galvanized my attention and opened my heart. It reminded me of Fred Rogers on his TV show telling us that "the best thing we can do for each other is to listen with our ears and our hearts" and Thich Nhat Hahn's concept of deep listening.

Being listened to without being interrupted, contradicted, or corrected was something I seldom experienced during my childhood beyond the time I lived with my grandparents after they were given temporary custody of me. As a result, I had come to believe that my thoughts and feelings were not important, were not valid, and so I developed a habitual pattern—both consciously and unconsciously—of suppressing myself.

Though I experienced no major transformational breakthrough during that initial three-day retreat, I felt more open in a new way. I was energized and activated by the process, and I knew that I wanted to go deeper. I left feeling grateful for the structure, the precision of the schedule, the simple yet delicious and mindfully prepared food, and the attentive, caring staff. It was the most potent and promising tool for growth I had encountered.

In the months that followed, I participated in several more of these unique three-day meditation retreats called Self-Realization or Enlightenment Intensives. During one that was held in a beautiful forested area in central California, I was using "Tell me what you are" as the instruction I received from each dyad partner. Toward the end of the second day, it became clear to me that there was one participant in the small group whom I was avoiding. I decided to confront whatever was making me hesitant to partner with that individual and sat down opposite him.

Halfway through our dyad, my physical body seemed to expand beyond any discernible form, and then disappear entirely. At the same time, my mind went completely blank. It then seemed as if I somehow merged with the being sitting opposite me. There was no discernible perception of the two of us, at the core level of reality, being in any way different or separate. Whatever I was and whatever he was, it was the same, and it had nothing to do with our bodies, our gender or our ego identifications. In the midst of this undeniable recognition, I gradually became aware of being both inside and outside of an ephemeral physical form. Unexpectedly, some remarkably bright phenomenon arose in the form of seeing ribbons of golden-tinged light coming out of the top of my head and joining with the same light coming out of my partner's head. Time and space and words became non-existent. I was truly speechless.

This inexplicable, yet unequivocal, experience changed my relationship with others. It was as if I'd been wearing sunglasses that had been suddenly removed. I began seeing other people in a completely new and different way. I perceived a sameness between myself and all others at an intrinsic level that had nothing to do with physical appearance, gender, personality, background, or disposition. I began to want to treat people better after that—not from some teaching that said I should, but from what I had actually experienced.

About a year later, I completed a rigorous, ten-day training course to learn how to lead this particular type of structured and intense meditative retreat. In a dyad during one of the practice periods, something occurred that caught me by surprise. The only word I could think of to describe it was innocence, an awareness that I was innocent. It was as if a ray of sunshine had landed on and in me, briefly. I didn't consciously connect it, at that time, with my birth mother's rejection of me or the fact that her actions had nothing to do with me. I just noticed that I was a little less restricted in some way; there was a small shift in my belief that I was never going to be "good enough."

By the end of that course, I knew I had met a teacher—not in the sense of some sort of guru or elevated being—but a person with integrity and wisdom who would mentor me in developing my ability to share this unique process that I sensed intuitively would lead me to reclaiming some essential part of myself that I had lost.

The following year, my husband completed the same training. He gave an inspiring three-day Intensive with the passion and skill of a natural-born teacher and with certainty born of his own experience with the technique being taught. He then became a crucial and dependable assistant for me as I continued organizing and leading such events.

During that same time period, I participated in a two-week Enlightenment Intensive held in our home. In my contemplation, I soon came face-to-face with personality traits in myself that I hadn't been consciously aware of—my criticalness, my hypocrisy, my need to be in control, my obsessive concerns about the environment. In the daily lectures, we were urged to be open and willing to go forward beyond the predictable, beyond what we were already conscious of. I continued facing my ego attachments, and fixations such as wanting my life to look good, wanting to be seen as a good parent, a good mate, a good person.

By the beginning of the second week, my inner critic seemed unstoppable. I had fallen into abject sorrow I could hardly bear as I re-experienced the deep shame, regret, and remorse I still carried regarding the failure of my first marriage. I became aware of how completely unconscious and unprepared I had been when I married while still in my teens. I actually thought that getting married meant I'd always be happy, be taken care of, be cherished. I assumed my husband would become my best friend and my ally in life. The reality of my physical and emotional loneliness in the relationship often felt like abandonment. I didn't believe my feelings were valid. Surely I wasn't giving enough or I wanted or expected too much. Even when both of us stepped outside the relationship into intimate encounters with other people, I was convinced it only happened because there was something lacking in me. If I had been a better person—more patient, more mature, had fewer expectations—then everything would have been fine.

A few days later, I was confronted with a pounding headache unlike anything I had ever encountered. It felt as if needles were being stuck into my eyeballs against my will. By evening, I was feeling sick to my stomach as well. Simply sitting upright was difficult, and staying in contact with my dyad partners seemed close to impossible. I felt shitty, weak, ugly, and as if I was being tortured. This physical state continued through most of the next day until it vanished as mysteriously as it had begun without the aid of any drug or therapeutic intervention.

Pushing through pain, fears, tears, distractions, energy fluctuations, and my habitually self-critical mind, I persisted with the practice, one day at a time. During the last one-hour walking contemplation period, I was moving slowly along the sidewalk on a nearby block, noticing trees, grasses, flowing plants, the sky, the clouds, even the houses I was passing as if I was seeing them for the first time. They appeared more defined, more colorful, more vibrant. The air smelled fresh and clean as if it has just rained. At some point I became aware of a baby wailing, as though in distress, which stopped me in my tracks. It seemed as if I was that baby. Was that how I had sounded to the neighbors whose reports finally led to the police breaking into my birth mother's apartment and my being rescued?

As the crying continued, my mind shifted; I began thinking about a very conscious decision I had made, before remarrying, not to have another child. After a long effort to persuade me to change my mind, my now husband had eventually accepted my decision. A stream of words abruptly broke through my thoughts, appearing like large letters on a chalkboard in my brain: "To be free you must be willing to be wrong about everything." The words kept repeating themselves until it seemed my head would explode. At that moment, I let go of my preconceived ideas, my desires, my certainty. I just laid that burden down. I metaphorically fell to my knees in the middle of an uneven sidewalk with little shoots of green grass growing up through the cracks and surrendered everything I thought I knew.

· · · · ·

The first Enlightenment Intensive I had attended became an annual event held at various retreat centers in northern California. I continued to take part in those once-a-year gatherings, either as participant, an assistant, or the facilitator/leader. One year, as a participant, while sitting opposite my partner during one of the last dyads of the three days, something extraordinary occurred. The light in the room changed perceptibly. It became brighter, yet softer—a golden, warm, protective glowing light—and I sensed my deceased father's presence. Simultaneously, dozens of celestial-like, beings seemed to fill the large, barn-like space we were in. I saw them clearly in my inner vision; I sensed the purity of their nature. They were everywhere. There was nowhere they were not. It was as if some invisible veil had lifted, allowing me to experience something that had been there all along.

Struggling to communicate to my dyad partner what was happening, I was flooded with emotion, along with the realization that nobody had ever not wanted me to experience the love that was flooding the room at that moment, and that was also inside me. I had never completely opened to the undeniable reality that was penetrating my being. I had never truly been alone. I had never not been who and what I am. I simply didn't have that truth mirrored to me during a crucial time in my life when the absence of a consistent, responsive and loving relationship was a serious threat to my neurological and cognitive development.

This experience was life-altering for me. It helped set me on a path toward liberating myself from the effects of my birth mother's abusive neglect and failure to claim me, and from the subsequent turmoil and uncertainty in my early childhood. It began to erode the deep-seated beliefs buried in my subconscious that I would never be enough, that I was inherently flawed somehow and didn't deserve to be truly loved because the woman who brought me into this world left me. I couldn't really live from that idea anymore. I still had vestiges of it, and a number of years would pass before those would dissolve completely, yet that false belief was no longer as deeply fixed in my being.

On a slightly different type of meditative retreat, while sweeping the floors during a working contemplation period, I was suddenly struck with an unadulterated and absolute revelation. No matter where my eyes landed—whether on another individual, a pair of shoes, a tree outside the window—absolutely everything I could see or touch had the same ineffable energy or quality. In that moment, I wanted nothing more than to bow to every person, to everything I laid eyes on. Sweeping the floor and lining up the shoes by the door was suddenly not a task to be completed in a mindful way; it was a natural action of pure joy in serving others.

I found myself in a blessedly blissful bubble for the rest of that day. The following day, however, I was plunged into an opposite state of being as all my mental baggage began to intrude. Struck by how out of touch I was, in my normal life, with the actuality I had experienced, it seemed to me that the effort to live my life in harmony with that truth was like trying to walk forward while buried in mud. My failure to consistently treat others as what they actually are seemed to me the equivalent of constantly spitting in the face of God. I quickly fell into deep and utter despair. I communicated this in private to the person leading the retreat who listened compassionately before reminding me that the truth itself doesn't change or go away. "You might forget about it or bury it in the mud, yet it is always there."

My understanding of the contemplative technique I was practicing and teaching gradually increased. I came to appreciate more and more the power in the reciprocal gift of being fully present for another, and completely open to another without interior monologue, and in turn, being received and heard in the same receptive, non-judgmental way. I began to understand that it is okay to feel however I feel, to understand that thoughts are simply thoughts, emotions are just emotions, and both are continually changing, much like the clouds or the weather. Over time, I was able, at least occasionally, to observe the constant chatter of my monkey mind, as I might view passing clouds in the sky, without evaluating, denying, or identifying with each thought that arose. I am gradually getting better at opening to whatever is arising, with less resistance, less judging, less labeling.

. . . . .

A number of years ago, my husband and I were offered a private audience with the head priest of a Jodo ("Pure Land School") Buddhist temple near Kamakura, Japan. Before meeting him, a vision had appeared in my head of a bare room with an old man sitting cross legged on a pillow, who might ask us a few questions without answers and dismiss us. Instead, we walked into a small room with a large and cluttered desk taking up at least half the space. The man behind the desk, wearing thick glasses, rose to greet us, smiling as if we were old friends, and motioned for us to sit on the chairs on the other side of his desk. He rang a small bell and soon a tray of tea and small cakes arrived, delivered by a robed monk who set the platter down carefully in front of us, then backed out of the room while bowing to our host.

Despite his high status in that community, Fukiyoshi Sensei could not have been more open and gracious, welcoming us amicably, as if he had nothing else to do. Fully present and attentive in his contact, he seemed to take much delight in telling us stories, speaking in a mix of English and Japanese, and chuckling often. When my husband shared a little bit about the experiences we were having from our participation in Enlightenment Intensives, the Sensei smiled sweetly at us and casually said something profound: "Oh yes, yes, such realizations are good, very nice, but the important thing is how they affect one's behavior in life. Do they help you treat others better?"

Our then seven-month-old daughter, who had been sitting quietly and wide-eyed in my lap, had not taken her eyes off our host. As he fixed his attention on her, my husband reflected briefly on our child exhibiting a strong ego. Sensei made a comment about her innocence before saying that, "as our egos develop, we start becoming critical and making judgments, but a strong sense of self is important in order to one day surrender to the Formless One." I have recalled our encounter with this great soul, and some of his words, many times over the years.

Though I had never consciously taken any vow to do so, and certainly blundered a few times along the way, I was able to bond with and care for my two older children in a way that my birth mother had been unable to do with me. When I was blessed with the third child, who was sitting on my lap that day, after two miscarriages on the way to meeting her, I felt I had been given a chance to parent in a more conscious and mindful way, to more deeply appreciate the gift of motherhood. My older daughter would later say in an interview that she felt she and her brother were mothered with the same love and attention I was giving to her younger sister, but that I was experiencing being a mother differently because of a change inside me.

·····

There are different paths to awakening, along with myriad myths and misconceptions in regard to enlightenment, or to "seeing into one's true nature." For some individuals, an awakened state occurs as a seemingly random and unexpected seismic shift in consciousness, or a quantum leap from one level of awareness to another. For others, it is a gradual unfolding over time. Awakening is not the end result of some arduous journey that leads to perfection or everlasting serenity, nor is it the end of adversity, or life challenges. We still inhabit human bodies; we still have minds and preferences and personalities. In many ways, our experiences of waking up to the reality of our connection to all beings, and all things is the beginning of a journey rather than an end of one.

I am now able to notice my thoughts and my emotions as they occur without getting attached to them, at least some of the time. Life continues to teach me. Parenting is a spiritual practice, marriage is a spiritual practice, surviving a life-threatening illness is a spiritual practice, staying present, no matter what circumstance we find ourselves in, is a spiritual practice. Truly, there is not one moment in our lives that is not an opportunity for deeper awakening.

Gazing out the window to the right of my desk, my fingers rest on the keyboard as I pause to look out at the sly, the sassy squirrels scampering across the rooftops and leaping into the nearby trees or the sparrows and chickadees somersaulting through the air. As I marvel at the effortless movement of a lone hawk, gliding on thermal currents, the rose bushes bursting into glorious color, the ever-changing shapes of snowy-white clouds moving slowly across a deep blue firmament or, occasionally, catch sight of a full moon slowly rising above the treetops, I am sometimes graced with an experience of union and peace that is truly beyond understanding.

> The moon's the same
>   old moon,
> The flowers exactly as
>   they were,
> Yet I've become the
>   thingness
> Of all the things I see!
>   —Shido Bunan

Lessons from the Elderly, the Ill, and the Dying

Compassion is much more than kind counsel or warm feelings—it's a natural, appropriate response to being in the presence of suffering.
—Frank Ostaseski

When you feel yourself to be a vehicle of kindness, an instrument of love, there is more to the deed than the doer and what's been done, you yourself feel transformed.

—Stephen Levine

After suffering two miscarriages in my early forties, my husband and I were deeply grateful to help usher a new being into this world during my forty-third year of life. Already teaching English and Humanities full time, my husband took on a second job teaching classes at a community college at night so that I could work full time as a stay-at-home mom. It was a role and a commitment that I found profoundly satisfying as well as enormously exhausting at times.

After about a year and a half, my husband noted that my contributions to our conversations at the end of his work day were becoming a bit—shall we say—limited. We began talking about ways that I might be able to exercise other parts of my brain by doing something new and creative just for myself. This led to my enrolling in a nearby graduate school where I intended to work slowly toward a degree in Counseling Psychology. As often happens in life, I was led in a different direction. A new certification program entitled "Awakening to Life and Death" got my attention, in large part because my father had recently been diagnosed with inoperable, metastasized lung cancer.

A component in completing the certification was an internship of sorts that required spending time on a weekly basis with at least one individual nearing death. I accomplished this by becoming a hospice volunteer, which allowed me to adapt my massage therapy and listening skills to being with those approaching the end of their lives.

In the meantime, my oldest daughter was carving out a career for herself working in residential care facilities. She mentioned that residents in the extended care center where she was then serving as their Social Services Director, could benefit from the type of auxiliary support I was offering to hospice patients. She pointed out that some family members would likely be happy to pay for that kind of amenity, adding that residents on MediCal, the California equivalent of Medicare, received a small discretionary monthly stipend that often went unspent.

Inspired by my daughter's idea, I created COMPASSIONATE TOUCH for those in Later Life Stages™ in order to reach out to groups of people who are often marginalized in our society, especially and specifically, the frail elderly, the chronically ill, and those nearing death. I wanted to serve individuals who are less mobile, who might be confined to wheelchairs or beds, and those alienated from the outside world, whether in their own homes or in care communities. I hoped to offer gentle massage and skilled touch to men and women who might be physically touched as part of routine caregiving, or in the course of medical tests and procedures, yet were seldom receiving the kind of nurturing, unconditional contact that I knew could be enormously comforting, and healing in the deepest sense.

I quickly discovered that my visits were especially needed and appreciated by those unable to clearly articulate their needs, whether due to a brain insult such as Alzheimer's Disease or other types of dementia, an inability to make themselves understood in English, or because the person had simply given up trying to talk when it became clear that nobody was really listening. Human hearts of all ages and in all situations yearn for acceptance, affection and authentic human connection. When words fail, touch continues the conversation. Intentional, yet non-invasive, physical contact offers comfort, support and assurance that a person is not alone.

As I began visiting residents in nursing homes and other care facilities, I was amazed at the positive indicators I received. I soon discovered that focused, conscious touch—along with open-hearted presence, and attentive listening—had enormous potential to ease discomfort, calm the mind and lift the spirit of the individuals I was spending time with. I learned that those who don't answer questions quickly enough or who may not respond to what they hear as repetitive or perfunctory comments from a busy caregiver such as "How are we feeling today?" or "Are you ready for your bath?" are often too quickly assumed to be nonverbal. Once that notation is in the resident's chart, other caregivers often stop making any effort to elicit a response.

Something completely unexpected came to light one day while I was visiting a woman in her mid-eighties who was living out her years in a long-term care facility. This tall, bone-thin, wheelchair-bound woman had not spoken a word during the several months I had been seeing her regularly, though after only a few bi-monthly visits, she had begun to make eye contact and return my smile as I was sitting with her, applying lotion to her hands and lower arms. Over time, she began to visibly relax her body as I gently massaged her shoulders and upper back. One day, completely out of the blue, this elder suddenly said quite clearly: "My husband and I used to go dancing." Startled, yet delighted to hear her voice, I asked where she and her husband liked to dance. She then described the venue in detail, and went on to answer, with increasing enthusiasm, every question I asked her! Grateful to know that she could still retrieve pleasant memories and share them, and that she trusted me with her words that morning, I was reluctant to leave her room. I never again let the designation of "nonverbal" speak for itself. It was not the last time I discovered the label to be an error.

My experience in spending time on a near daily basis for several years with my mother, Ruth Ann, and later, my mother-in-law, as each woman moved from a home she had lived in for decades to assisted living, to nursing care, to board and care, and eventually, to hospice care, afforded me new insights. I gained a greater awareness of the vicissitudes of life for those who have little control over their environments—the sounds, the sights, the smells, the schedule—and who become powerless to change their situations. Being present with each of these women in the last stages of a long life, and as each drew her last breath, was an additional gift.

It is not unusual to see residents in care facilities, sitting in their rooms or in hallways, virtually unnoticed and ignored by busy, and often overworked and underpaid caregivers. "Just waiting . . . waiting . . . waiting," a resident in her wheelchair opposite the nurse's station once uttered softly when I stopped to ask her how she was doing that day. Facility residents like her are often literally waiting—sometimes for what must seem like hours—for someone to smile at them, to say hello, to call them by name, to acknowledge their existence. My gradual familiarity with a number of those residents provided me with indisputable evidence of the efficacy of mindful contact, of even a few minutes of listening without an agenda, without evaluating, without giving advice or administering medications.

The frail elderly, the chronically ill and those nearing the end of their lives can feel abandoned in a multitude of ways as they experience never-to-be-reversed losses, sometimes in quick succession. Such individuals can find themselves in facility care for any number of reasons. Some need rehabilitation after an injury; others need short-term care while recovering from surgery. Others have been relocated because family members believe their loved ones can no longer live alone safely, or because they have no family members who are both able and willing to provide the kind of support their loved ones have come to need.

Regardless of the reasons for such a move, leaving one's home and familiar surroundings represents a major lifestyle change. That aging or ill individual is suddenly bereft of familiar surroundings, relegated to rules and timetables, for everything from food service to entertainment and group activities, based on management efficiency and convenience of administrators and staff members rather than on individual preferences, habits, rhythms, and tastes. Stress, anxiety, and depression are common in such communities, and are nearly always treated with prescription drugs which, in turn, have their own side effects.

I have long remembered a cheerful, wheelchair-bound woman I spent time with once a week at a respite care center. She was one of the more alert and talkative women in the program and usually greeted me with a big smile. One day, even before I sat down beside her, I noticed that she seemed to be upset about something. When I touched her arm and asked her what was wrong, she whispered tearfully, "I don't live in my house anymore." I kept my attention on her, holding her hand until she continued. She said that, without giving her any warning, her daughters were moving her into "one of those facilities." According to her, her daughters told her she would be there for just a few days, and then she discovered the move was to be permanent.

When I was able to get permission to visit this woman in the nursing home she'd been moved to, I found her struggling to adjust to a completely new, unfamiliar environment among strangers. She was, understandably, feeling confined, with only a few of her personal belongings, in a much smaller space than she was used to, and which she was sharing with a woman she'd never met before (mentioning that her roommate kept her awake at night with her loud snoring). From her point of view at least, she'd had no say in the decision that was made on her behalf. I validated what she was feeling and told her I was sorry. I tried not to judge her daughters, realizing that I was privy to a very small part of what was likely a much larger story.

From my present perspective, I can see that my childhood experience of being placed in an institutional care setting, with little understanding or power over the situation, instantly relegated to life among strangers in an unfamiliar environment, provided a context for empathy and compassion to germinate and grow in me. I realized much later that the fulfillment I receive from relating to those in the later stages of life comes from my ability to offer the support I did not have during that lonely and vulnerable time in my early childhood.

I don't have the ability to change a person's circumstances or condition. I cannot be a "savior." I am unable to reverse an aging or a disease process, nor can I change a medical system or a family dynamic. What I can do is recognize and acknowledge the individual and be present with him or her. I can remain conscious, open and kind during whatever time we spend together.

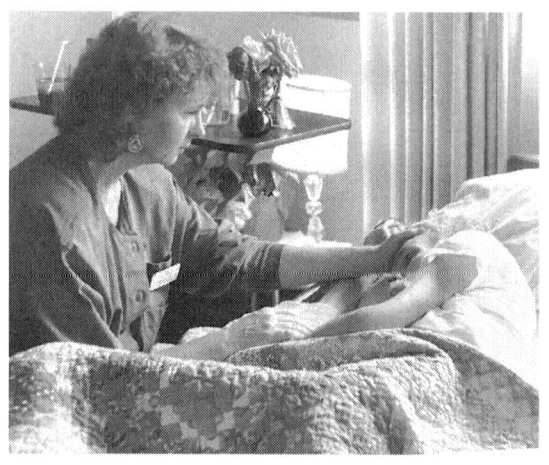

In my years of working regularly with individuals nearing death, I was often particularly moved by my encounters with those suffering from AIDS. Not all were male, nor were they all gay, yet invariably they were much younger than other men and women I was seeing. Often in their twenties or thirties, some were angry, some were afraid, some were bitter. Many were isolated and lonely.

One young man I spent time with had been abandoned by both parents and his two brothers, due to his "lifestyle choices." When I met him, he was withdrawn and dispirited. Beneath his depression, I could see a scared young boy crying out for his mother, longing for acceptance from his father, and mourning the loss of companionship he might have had with his brothers. After only a few visits, he told me he was ready to die, and that he wished he could speed up the process. I knew from the one sibling who had remained in his life, the sister who was caring for him, that their mother—in defiance of her husband—was coming to see him. I gently suggested maybe he could give his mom a chance.

Portals to Awakening

I happened to be the only other person in the home the day his mother came to the door, suitcase in hand, planning to stay for a few weeks. She was so clearly distressed and anxious, as she stepped into the house that I spontaneously hugged her. As she held me tightly for a long minute, I felt her enormous sorrow as well as the courage it took for her to be there, her love swallowing her terror. We shared a few words, one mother to another, before I ushered her into the room where her son lay in his bed, emaciated and distant. I have always hoped that they achieved some form of reconciliation in the three days they gave each other before her life-weary child let go of his body.

As the inspiring author/physician, Rachel Naomi Remen says, "It is our wounds that enable us to be compassionate with the wounds of others." I know now that choosing to interact with men and women who are often secluded, lonely, and anxious, has been a profound and powerful way of helping me heal from those early periods of my life when I experienced a number of the same feelings—when I was vulnerable, when I longed to be noticed and listened to, when I was in need of acknowledgement, nourishing touch, and caring attention.

The simplest, yet all too often ignored, acts of kindness, compassion, and authentic contact can deeply affect both the giver and the receiver. Even a few moments of deep listening, combined with nonintrusive, gentle touch, can truly make a difference. I have witnessed this countless times over the years.

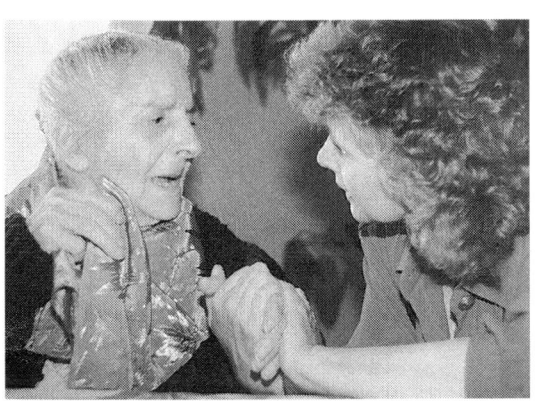

Each person I have been privileged to meet during this unique period in his or her life has taught me something new about myself, about life, about aging, about death, about love, about surrender. The emotional impact and notable lessons from many of those interactions are detailed in my book, *From the Heart Through the Hands: The Power of Touch in Caregiving*. Suffice it to say that a few situations have been mentally and emotionally draining. Some have been intense, initially awkward or uncomfortable, while others were relaxing, tranquil, inspiring, sacred. Some of the environments I've encountered have been cluttered and chaotic while others were calm, peaceful, spaces. I visited a few individuals only once or twice. Others I spent time with regularly for weeks or months, or, in a few instances, over a year or longer. Sometimes other family members were present and were included in my sessions; other times the person I was sent to see was alone.

My interactions with individuals approaching death continue to remind me that we can find sweetness in unexpected people and places, that life itself, to the extent that we are open to it, is "the lesson" and that every moment of life and death is holy. Whether the person I am contacting is five years old, or 101, I try my best to surrender my ego, to trust my instincts, and to rise above my fatigue or fear in order to be present with, and for, another during a fragile and vulnerable time in his or her life. The scores of individuals who have allowed me to touch their bodies, to listen to their stories, to sit awhile with them, and to share their precious time have enriched my life, expanded my awareness of impermanence, and deepened my capacity for compassion. My work with the elderly, the ill and the dying has challenged me, changed me, and brought me into deeper contact with my true self.

My stepmother, Ruth Ann, also known as Ruth, Ruthie, and occasionally R.A., once told me that her parents had considered naming her Esther.

Chapter Ten

Forgiving Esther

Forgiveness is the necessary ground for any healing. Sometimes it's quick and sometimes it takes a lifetime.

—Jack Kornfield

Forgiveness is the most powerful healer of them all.

—Gerald G. Jampolsky

"Forgive Esther for what exactly?" one might ask. For starters, for the humiliation, the emotional blackmail, the harassing, haranguing, criticizing and "opinionating" me to death; for forever trying to make me be something better, something else, something more, or something different from what I was; for the incessant—and I do mean incessant, as in constant, continuous, unending, ceaseless, interminable, perpetual and everlasting—preachy harping; for the seemingly endless stream of words that poured out of her mouth, infiltrating my being, clogging every pore in my body until I could hardly breathe, filling every mental air pocket in my brain until my own embryonic thoughts were suffocated mid-birth.

Nearly every day that Esther and I spent together in the same house, I went to sleep to the sound of her voice and awoke to the same sound whether she was talking to me, to someone else, or to herself. It didn't seem to matter to her if people were listening to what she was saying or if they talked back. When she asked a question, she seemed unable to keep her mouth from moving long enough to listen to the answer.

During my youth, one of the few times Esther stopped talking was when she was sunbathing. It was as if the heat incinerated her words before they could escape from her mouth. On sunny days she would rush home from her secretarial job, set up the folding aluminum and vinyl chaise lounge in our small backyard, take off her blouse, pull up her skirt, and stretch out to catch whatever rays she could. After a friend told her that putting a drop or two of iodine in Johnson's Baby Oil was the best way to get a fast tan, she religiously applied this potion to her exposed skin. In lieu of sunglasses, Esther placed wet, flattened cotton balls over her eyelids. I never knew if she was asleep under those white pallets, mulling over plans for the future, or simply daydreaming. As the days shortened in the fall, Esther had less and less time in the sun, but when spring moved towards summer, my respite from her words might lengthen to an hour or more.

Apart from talking, Esther's favorite pastime seemed to be clothes shopping. As a child, I was often forced to accompany Esther on long and tedious excursions in which I became her "runner," making endless trips between the dressing room and the racks to exchange one piece of clothing for another in a different size or color. Like most decisions Esther made, choosing which items to purchase was never quick or simple. Her choices came only after a long, meandering, incomprehensible-to-anyone-but-her dialogue that Esther's mind carried on, sometimes out loud, with itself.

Esther's presence in any department store inevitably meant there was a sale in progress. Picture gaggles of women of all ages, shapes and sizes hell-bent on snatching the best possible deal before anyone else can grab it, descending like birds of prey on the pocketed wooden tables filled with seasonal attire, pecking at whatever bits of color or fabric catch their fancy until the neatly ordered piles turn into one big blur of tossed and tousled material. Clutching their prizes in brightly polished talons as if their lives depended on it, the crazed creatures then move quickly to the racks of dresses, slacks, or skirts, their minds and eyes intently focused on the hunt, their squawks turning shrill as they compete with each other for the attention of the sales girls or argue with shopping partners about the merits of one color or style over another. This escalating vocal cacophony, combined with the distinctive whoosh of the cash-stuffed tubes moving through the pneumatic tube system on their way to the cashiers, creates a din that assails the senses of anyone not involved in the frenzy.

I once sought refuge in the center of a large circular rack only to discover a like-minded young person. The pig-tailed, freckle-faced girl forgave me for invading her secret cave, grinning conspiratorially as we both hid from the madding crowd. We sat smugly and silently, like two escapees from Leavenworth as the garments swished and whirled around us until we were discovered, duly chastised, and dragged off by our forearms, in opposite directions.

Occasionally, two women—one of them being Esther—would reach for the same item at the same time. When this occurred, Esther resorted to one of two tactics. The first was to declare, in a cloyingly sweet yet raised voice, "Oh I'm so sorry dear, but I had this first," while smiling meaningfully and keeping a firm grip on the item until the other woman dropped her end. Her alternate strategy was to accost the offending shopper in a loud, accusing voice. "Hey, what are you trying to pull? You saw me reaching for this one!" or "You know I had this first!" The accompanying facial expression was a piercing, beady-eyed look under furrowed brows. If all else failed, Esther would just give an unexpected yank and end the contest.

Once Esther managed to make up her mind regarding which items she wanted, there was still the line to wait through before her selections could be purchased or put on layaway. As I stood beside Esther in the row of chattering women, she would invariably spot some garment she hadn't noticed before in her mad dash through the racks, or become plagued with doubt about a choice she'd made, and I was left to hold her place in line while she rushed back into the fray.

Whether due to my height, my age or my silence, the buyers behind me in the ever-lengthening queue usually ignored me as if I was wearing an invisibility cloak as they continued their forward movement. More often than not, Esther was so preoccupied with her decision-making process that she failed to notice I had gained little if any ground by the time she returned.

The annual Henry's Clothing and Shoe Store event held every December seemed to excite Esther at least as much as Christmas. Esther never missed this chance to save money and stock up on shoes, most of which she would never wear. At that point in her life, Esther could dazzle, bewitch, or seduce nearly any man into giving her whatever she wanted with a simple turn of turn of her head and an enigmatic smile. I watched, with a mixture of fascination and embarrassment, as she flirted with the young salesmen sitting on their wooden shoe-fitting stools in front of her, easing her silk stockinged feet into shoe after shoe. With each new offering, Esther would parade before them, inviting their thoughts as to which pair of shoes looked better. The smart ones would say that every shoe looked so good on her, they just couldn't decide, at which point Esther would laugh playfully and say if that were the case, she supposed she'd just have to take both pairs, and two more boxes would be added to the growing stack.

. . . . .

Racing towards thirteen, I was wearing my recently acquired real bra, desperately wishing I was older and sitting anywhere other than the passenger side of Esther's old black Plymouth sedan, when she abruptly made one of her impulsive "stop even though there is no sale going on" maneuvers at a local department store. Once inside, Esther waved me over to the section displaying clothing that might soon fit my quickly changing body, telling me I could "browse" for a few minutes.

The navy-blue skirt stood out like a jewel in gravel. There were few people in that area of the store that weeknight, and no sales girl in sight as I lifted the hanger from its rack and boldly headed for a dressing room. This remarkable piece of clothing, a fitted skirt made of some sort of seductively soft yet durable material, fit perfectly around my newly forming hips. The smooth, silk-like lining caressed my legs when I moved. Words cannot describe the sensations I experienced gazing at my image in the full-length mirror. It was as if the skirt possessed some supernatural power that made me appear not only older but prettier, smarter, happier. I begged Esther to buy it for me and in the end, most likely distracted by her own decision-making process, she consented.

I wore the magical garment to the next Wednesday-night prayer meeting at our church. Esther sat down near the back and, without waiting for permission, I walked all the way up to the front pews where the young people were encouraged to sit. I could literally feel both the song leader and the preacher looking at me differently. The boy who would become my first kiss a few months later came right up to me at the end of the service and mumbled something I chose to hear as a prelude to romance.

The next day, without warning or discussion, Esther removed the skirt from my closet and returned it to the store. I never knew the exact reason she changed her mind, but I hated her for the betrayal, and I vowed I would never forgive her. Perhaps she felt somehow threatened by my emerging sexuality. Maybe noticing how people had glanced at me made her feel she'd be judged in some way. Or, just possibly, it nudged Esther into the realization that I was growing up and would one day move beyond her control. She needn't have worried. Her invasion of my being was so complete that it took me decades to begin truly thinking for myself.

As I neared my mid-teens, Esther was becoming more and more religious, my father was spending more and more time out of town, and I was on the receiving end of Esther's frustration and resentment. Thankfully, I was allowed to attend a boarding school in another state to escape the fallout when my father took his leave of Esther and began spending more time with the woman who would become his fourth and final wife.

With my father and I both gone, Esther sought prayers and counseling. Eventually rallying after what was referred to as her nervous breakdown, she flew to Paris to visit a friend, and procured a Civil Service job that kept her living abroad for two decades. Far away from her former life, Esther fell off the church pew and reinvented herself. By changing her hair color, the way she dressed, and the birth date on her passport, she was able to successfully present herself as ten years younger than she actually was. Esther learned to ski, traveled every chance she got, and dated a steady stream of men of varying ages.

. . . . .

When Esther retired from her overseas job and moved back to the town where we had once lived together, she sent me a plane ticket to come see her. She insisted on spending the first day of my three-day visit going to the end-of-summer department store sales. Her habits little changed, she draped my arms with "outfits" for one of us to try on, chirping on in a mostly one-way conversation about what tops went best with which bottoms. Digging through the sales bins at a frenzied pace, something that had surely always been inevitable occurred. Esther and another sales addict grabbed a gauzy, white blouse at the same moment.

Like two birds with one worm, they each yanked and the material ripped. There was a brief hush, in a stop-motion millisecond, before the other shoppers quickly dispersed. Apparently at a loss for words—for possibly the second time in her life—Esther quickly released her grip on the material and strode silently toward the nearest store exit, with me at her heels.

Esther's conversion to a radically different way of shopping was swift. Secondhand stores offered the ultimate, never ending sale, and they were seldom overcrowded. In the years to come, Esther's Christmas boxes arrived filled with carefully wrapped and ribboned gifts of pre-owned clothing that might or might not fit anyone in our family, children's books with at least one torn or missing page, jigsaw puzzles absent the final piece, or toys lacking some crucial part.

During Esther's visits "out west," perusing our local thrift shops was high on her agenda. It mattered little to Esther if the clothes she bought were her size. If something caught her eye or appealed to her in any way, she'd snatch it, deciding later what to keep for herself and what to give to someone else. I learned to simply thank Esther for any purchases passed on to me or my family, taught my children to do the same, and donated most of the items back to the same thrift store later.

Esther's long-distance telephone conversations were no different from those she carried on in person. I once prepared an entire meal during one of her seemingly unlimited calls. When I needed both hands, I set the telephone receiver down on the kitchen counter, leaning over every so often to murmur, "Hmm," "Oh?" or "Really!" This was about all that was required from my end for a good half hour or more.

. . . . .

As fate would have it, I chose to take responsibility for Esther's care and well-being during what turned out to be the last two years of her life. When I suggested a move to California, she told everyone in the Midwestern nursing home—where she had been living an underactive and overmedicated life—that she was going to "the land of sunshine," where fresh fruit and vegetables were plentiful year-round, to be nearer to her grandchildren and to meet "my grand-dogs and grand-cats!"

Age had begun taking its toll on Esther, though she could still talk a blue streak on a good day once she got started. She became stooped and her gait was unsteady until she accepted the walker she had sworn she would never use. Esther loved visiting the dog and cats in our home on weekends. She thrived on the attention bestowed upon her in the Assisted Living community not far from our house, making no distinction between her fellow residents in the building—including a cat—and the caregivers, befriending them all. She was thrilled with the variety of food served in the well-appointed dining room, especially the desserts.

Ignoring her infirmities, Esther flirted up a storm, sweet-talking the male servers assigned to her table just as she had the young men in Henry's shoe department decades before. She had no trouble cajoling an eager to please young man into bringing her extra ice cream or second servings of her favorite pies. She once advised the head chef, who strolled through the dining room every so often exuding a certain glib charm, that a bit of lemon juice on the steamed spinach would improve the taste, adding with a coquettish laugh that serving it with fried potatoes and onions would make it perfect.

After a middle-of-the-night fall and surgery for a broken hip, Esther had to be moved to a nearby nursing home for rehabilitation. I came most days during the lunch hour, often bringing foods I knew she liked, to coax her into eating more. No longer able to speak and consume food at the same time, Esther predictably chose talking over eating.

On warm days, I'd wheel Esther outside after lunch so she could sit in the sunshine she loved. She often pointed out things I hadn't noticed—birds frolicking in the courtyard fountain or gathered to gossip on a rooftop, unusual cloud shapes, a butterfly dining on salvia, or an iris about to unfurl. When she tired, Esther would simply close her eyes and turn her face toward the sun.

Esther spoke less and less as the months passed, sometimes going silent for long periods of time. Incredibly, I found myself missing the sound of her voice. Asking her questions brought limited responses, although bringing in pictures of her ancestors prompted stories I'd never heard before. Peering at those age-old black-and-white photographs seemed to jump-start her mind as she described the colors of the flowers in the background or details about the materials in the dress her "Mama stayed up nearly all night sewing" for her. Pausing one day, mid-sentence, a puzzled look crossed Esther's face. "Where are my sisters now?" she asked, as if she'd misplaced something precious. I searched my mind for an answer that would reassure rather than upset her.

"Why, they're in heaven, waiting for you, I expect."

"Oh, yes," Esther replied, smiling at me with such gratitude and childlike innocence that I couldn't look away.

"I love you, Mother." I heard myself say earnestly. Esther responded as if she might have been asking what day it was.

"Am I your mother?"

"Yes," I replied, with a long-delayed certainty, you are my mother."

The expression that appeared on Esther's face, the look in her eyes at that moment, was sweetness itself. I let my tears fall. I experienced a rush of heat over my entire body. And then, something extraordinary happened. It was as if Esther and I were suddenly in that field that mystics talk about, out beyond wrong doing and right doing. There was nothing to forgive. There was nothing but love in my heart. There was nothing but Love, period.

A few weeks later, my mother died in my arms as I sang her favorite hymn about Jesus calling her home. I substituted the word "loved one" for "sinner" in the chorus.

"Softly and tenderly, Jesus is calling, calling, oh loved one, come home."

Chapter Eleven

Goddess Descending: The Larger Story

Some people come into your life as blessings, others come into your life as lessons.
— Mother Theresa

Soul making requires that you die to one story to be reborn to a larger one.
— Jean Houston

In an exercise entitled "Healing the Sacred Wound" in Jean Houston's groundbreaking work, *The Search for the Beloved*, one is asked to focus on a significant upheaval or distress in her or his life, to answer certain questions about the event, and then to reimagine and rewrite the story by assuming the role of mythmaker, using archetypal images. Completing this assignment was the beginning of a shift in my perspective regarding the traumatic events that occurred during my infancy and early childhood.

I

In the realm of Eternal Light, there lived a Goddess known as Eos, the Goddess of the Rising Sun. After giving the matter a great deal of thought, Eos approached Hera, Queen of the Heavenly Realms, with a request that she be sent to a planet called Earth in the form of a human being.

"For what purpose?" she was asked.

"I want to understand Sorrow and Joy. I want to learn about Suffering, Eos explained, "and I have heard that human beings suffer most of all."

"Are you willing to stay on the Planet of Sorrows, in a human body and experience whatever is necessary to learn what you wish to?" asked the Queen of Heavenly Realms.

"I am," Eos replied.

"Then I will grant your wish, but I will need to find one willing to make the sacrifice to assist in this most difficult task."

The Goddess of the Rising Sun—who was not known for her patience—said resolutely, "I will wait."

It came to pass that Leto, the Goddess of Motherhood, volunteered to fulfill the request of Hera to help teach the Goddess of the Rising Sun about Suffering, Sorrow, and Joy.

Hera admonished Eos—who was often found floating dreamily in the heavenly realms while creating new light—to *Stay awake and pay attention!* "Although your father on Earth will become very important to you later in your life, it is the one who has consented to give birth to you in human form who will be the first to help teach you that which you seek to learn.

II

And so it was that the Goddess of the Rising Sun arrived on the planet called Earth, born through the body of a young female Earthling whose name was Grace. Becoming human was not easy. It required a long, uncomfortable struggle through a dark and narrow tunnel which seemed to cause the Earth woman great pain. As the Goddess of the Rising Sun tried to push her way out of the tunnel, she could feel resistance and fear surrounding her.

The human giving birth was put into a deep sleep so that she missed her baby's entrance onto the planet called Earth. She did not recognize the being who emerged from her body as who she actually was. The new Mother felt only disappointment when she recognized the infant who came through her body was a girl instead of the male child she thought she wanted. She resented the pain she had endured, and she was angry that the father of her child was far away in "The War" instead of being there with her. She wasn't even sure why she decided to call the infant "Dawn," though something deep inside her seemed to remind her of a task she had been given to carry out.

III

The Goddess of the Rising Sun becoming human was dependent on the Earth woman whose body she had emerged from to love and protect her, feed her, and keep her clean and warm, yet the human woman left her all alone much of the time. The baby called Dawn cried out when she was wet or cold or hungry for that is all her small body could do. Maybe the Earth woman couldn't hear her. When she cried louder, sometimes the woman came to the platform girded on all sides that humans called a crib, and lifted her out, yet many times no one came.

In due time, she was able to turn her small body over, and to move a little on her hands and knees. After a few more months of human time, she began trying to imitate some of the words human beings use to communicate with one another, which seemed to please her human Mother.

It came to pass during the time Earth beings call Autumn, that the human mother left her baby alone once again after darkness fell. This time, she was not there when the dark faded into light and then back to dark again. The human baby called Dawn was trapped and could do nothing to help herself. She cried as long and as loud as she could, yet nobody came. There was only darkness and light and then darkness once again. Each time she awoke she was hungrier and colder. As light turned to darkness once more, she grew weaker, and somewhere inside her, a feeling began to form that she had done something wrong. She began to lose touch with her small human body. Her energy waned and she could make no sound when the strangers came and found her.

A kind woman quickly put clean clothing on her, wrapped her in a blanket, and rushed her to a large space with bright lights and strange noises. After several days in this unfamiliar place, she was taken to the parents of her Earth Father's home where she was loved and nurtured and eventually began to thrive under her Grandparents' devoted, tender care. As she learned to walk and talk a little, she seemed to forget the dark wound in her soul and being forsaken by the woman who was her mother; yet the Goddess become mortal had a long journey ahead of her.

IV

In the course of Earth time, the human named Dawn grew into a woman. She came together with a human male who was good and kind and whom she promised to love and honor. She trusted that she was fulfilling her destiny on Earth. When she became a mother herself, the love she felt for the two beings who came through her body was greater than any she had ever known. If one of them suffered, she experienced the pain as her own and she also suffered.

Even though she made mistakes, the human on Earth called Dawn tried as hard as she could to be a good wife and a good mother. When the life she thought she was destined to live changed course, she believed she had failed and that she alone was to blame. She even thought that she did not deserve to be alive, yet her life on Earth continued. When she remembered the story about her first year of life and thought about the woman who had abandoned her, there was a deep sorrow inside her that never truly went away. She was convinced that she was not worthy of True Love.

Leto, the Goddess of Motherhood, who had left the Heavenly Realms to become human on Earth to help fulfill the request of the Goddess of the Rising Sun, lived a difficult life, struggling with shame, guilt, and the demons of addiction. Her heart was often heavy. After leaving her human body and returning to the Heavenly Realms, Leto was congratulated by Hera for the great skill she had displayed in carrying out her difficult assignment on the Planet of Sorrows known as Earth.

V

On the planet called Earth, it came to pass that the Goddess of the Rising Sun become human was united with another male Earthling who was persistent and determined in his quest to prove his unwavering love and support. In the fullness of time, they came together as life partners.

When the human called Dawn felt a deep yearning to give birth to one more child in her lifetime and her aging body rejected two beings sent into her womb, her Sorrow was great. The earnest supplications of Eos in her human form and her promise to pay close attention and to learn all that she could if she was allowed to give birth to one more child moved Hera, Queen of the Heavenly Realms.

When Leto, the Goddess of Motherhood approached Hera and asked to return to Earth one more time, both wishes were granted. The

Queen of the Heavenly Realm even sent her daughter, the Goddess of Pregnancy and Birth to watch over and protect the human named Dawn until her child arrived safely on the planet called Earth.

And so a new human life emerged, a radiant, pure and beautiful baby girl whose sweetness filled the room. The hearts of the human mother and father were opened and they were allowed to know that the child was a Divine being come to Earth to teach them something important. They honored her by remaining conscious of who she actually was, and by striving to be the best caretakers they possibly could, even when it was utterly fatiguing and their energy wavered.

As she grew, the child brought light and joy to the hearts of all who knew her. Her Mother thought that perhaps she was only able to appreciate the Joy she now felt because of the deep Sorrow carved into her being. She began to understand that she did deserve True Love and that it was actually something she had never been without.

The great wound began to heal. The Goddess of the Rising Sun become human on Earth opened her heart more and more to her True Self, to the Eternal Goodness and Love that is. Leto, the Goddess of Motherhood who had asked to be reborn on Earth, was now released from her previous agreement to teach the Goddess of the Rising Sun about Suffering. She was now free to express fully and completely the great love she had always felt for the human on Earth she had once named Dawn.

Chapter Twelve

Stepping Stones on the Path

Gratitude

It is through gratitude for the present moment that the spiritual dimension of life opens up.
—Eckhart Tolle

If the only prayer you ever say in your entire life is thank you, it will be enough.
—Meister Eckhart

The act of giving thanks, or a general state of appreciation and thankfulness, is the subject of countless articles, books, workbooks, blogs and podcasts expounding on the myriad benefits of such a practice, and revealing how an "attitude of gratitude" can change both our brains and our lives. Ongoing research continues to uncover a multitude of benefits accrued by intentional gratitude for as little as five minutes a day. The positive effects include lowering blood pressure and boosting the immune system, as well as improving self-esteem, enhancing empathy, strengthening relationships, combatting depression and helping people sleep better. Gratitude may also play a major role in healing from trauma.

Cultivating gratitude helps us navigate the bumpy roads of our lives and expands our perspective, allowing us to see a larger landscape. In short, practicing gratitude on a regular basis can have substantial and lasting effects. Thanks giving is a persuasive prescription for improving physical, mental, emotional, and spiritual health, while nurturing wholeness.

I spontaneously turned to gratitude as a support during my first four-hour chemotherapy treatment after undergoing surgery for ovarian cancer in 1998. Focusing on what I had to be grateful for was a godsend in the infusion room, when lying still for MRI or CT scans, or when I was trying to sleep in the middle of the night with peripheral neuropathy running rampant in my legs. That choice reinforced the lesson that the simple act of shifting our attention to focus on something that is available to us instead of thinking about what we don't have or cannot do has tremendous power over the mind. When I was too weak to walk around the block, I could be grateful to make it down our long driveway to the mailbox; when I didn't have the energy to prepare a meal for my family, I was grateful I could fix myself a cup of hot tea or cook a bowl of oatmeal for my breakfast.

During my illness, I became newly conscious of the long chain of hands and hearts that were contributing to my daily life and to my recovery process, beginning with my medical team, my family, and the student turned friend who voluntarily drove down from Oregon to stay with us during my first week home from the hospital, seeing to our every need with singular generosity and compassion. My gratitude for the food cooked for us and delivered by different families every few days in the following weeks extended beyond being thankful for the time those friends took to prepare and bring the meals. I was thankful I was able to sit up in a chair at the table and that I could see, smell, chew, swallow and digest the food. I became aware of how many people—from the farmhands to the harvesters to the packers to the truck drivers to the store owners to the grocery clerks—were collectively responsible for that food reaching my mouth, giving me nourishment, and contributing to my healing.

While slowly recovering my energy and brain power after my medical treatments ended, gratitude remained essential. Expressing gratitude for auxiliary therapies, for gifts of all kinds received from family and friends in such loving and creative ways, as well as gifts from nature, from the universe, and so on became a daily habit. From that time forward, I began each morning, while still in bed, by "counting my blessings." It took less than 10 minutes to think of 100 things to be grateful for though I soon quit keeping count of the number or the time. Gratitude helped calm my nerves on the way to the medical center for visits to my oncologist, during blood draws (especially when the needle didn't make its way into a vein on a first or second try) and for follow-up tests during that year.

In the months following the completion of my cancer treatments, I needed various kinds of dental work. Practicing gratitude during those necessary procedures not only helped get me to those anxiety-producing appointments on time, but gradually supported me in releasing the stress and anxiety I had carried most of my life associated with going to the dentist. I often sang out my gratitude list on the drive to the dentist's office, and silently generated another list during the procedures.

I have long remembered a lesson in gratitude I learned from a woman in her early thirties. As a result of a horseback-riding accident a few years before we met, she was living out her life as a quadriplegic in a long-term care home. Her mobility was severely limited yet her spirit seemed as vast as the sky. The day I met her in the care facility where I was giving a training workshop, she was reading a book, positioned on a special tray affixed to her chair. She was able, with concentrated effort, to turn the pages by using a device attached to her forehead. Her beautiful brown eyes smiled at me, even though her mouth couldn't. When I asked if she had enjoyed the touch she received from one of my students that day, she gave an enthusiastic, affirmative nod. Then, formulating the words slowly and with some difficulty, she said proudly, "Guess what? I can feel my legs!" The teaching she gave me in that moment in regard to focusing on what one has to be grateful for instead of on what is irretrievably lost was immense.

As my gratitude practice continued to deepen and expand, memories from my youth began to surface along with people whose names I'd long forgotten or situations I hadn't thought of in years. Names and images from my past began to appear in my consciousness like little lights twinkling in the darkness. I realized that these people were individuals who, in the trajectory of my life, had recognized something in me, behind my usual façade, people who actually saw *me*: my fourth-grade classroom teacher; my junior high homeroom teacher, my high school drama teacher; my college music teacher and his wife, an intuitive and skillful therapist I'd had only a few sessions with years before. Though I wasn't aware of it at the time, their recognition made a difference; each of these individuals, in their own way, provided me with a stepping stone on a long path to recovering my Self.

My gratitude practice carried me further and further back through the decades of my life until the day came when an unexpected thought appeared. "I am grateful to Penny, for carrying me inside her body for nine months and going through the painful process to bring me into this world." This recognition engendered an acute awareness of the fact that regardless of what happened after I was born, I would not be here today had she not given birth to me; and regardless of her persistent neglect during my first year of life, she did enough to keep me alive. I am grateful I didn't die.

Soon after that I was able to express gratitude for the fact that my birth mother drove from Florida to Kansas to meet me when I was seventeen, grateful to have met her when she was sober, grateful for my interactions with her a few more times across the years, grateful to have survived our visit when her sobriety had lapsed without anything disastrous occurring. I was grateful that she was able to "visit" me the night she died.

Upon learning the name of the woman responsible for obtaining the search warrant that led to my discovery and rescue, Laurel Lyons was added to my gratitude list. Though I'll never know their names, the neighbors who called in to report a crying baby unattended in a darkened apartment—once again perhaps—that particular night, have also been added to my gratitude list.

Gratitude isn't limited to a particular time or place. It can be practiced in nearly any setting: during dental procedures, standing in line at the post office; sitting in a waiting room before a medical appointment; lying in a hospital bed preparing for surgery; waiting for a stoplight to change from red to green; resting on a park bench; gazing through a window at a rose garden, or when having trouble getting to sleep. Our gratitude lists can be generated silently in the mind or be voiced out loud. They can be handwritten, typed, whispered, sung, chanted to the beat of a drum, rhymed, alphabetized, categorized, drawn, painted or collaged by oneself or with a group. The opportunities and possibilities are unlimited.

My personal gratitude exercise continued to deepen and expand as I shared it with loved ones, in group meetings, in friendship circles, and in training workshops. Any time I begin to feel tense, overwhelmed, distracted, irritable or frustrated, if I simply inhale and exhale deeply once or twice, and sit quietly for a moment, this focusing, calming practice begins without effort.

The act of expressing thanks can help support us as we navigate

unexpected challenges and changes in our lives, whether those difficulties are physical, mental, medical, emotional, or spiritual, whether it is a climate-related catastrophe or a worldwide pandemic blanketing our world, or the sudden loss of a loved one altering our day-to-day reality. Gratitude helps us refocus when we become distracted and get lost inside thoughts about the past or the future. It helps bring us back to the present moment, which is all we ever truly have. A consistent and purposeful acknowledgement of the gifts we so frequently take for granted, including the very fact of our existence on this earth, enlarges our perspective and adds grace to our days.
Breathing in I am alive. Breathing out I am grateful.

Blessing

To bless means to wish, unconditionally from the deepest chamber of your heart, unrestricted good for others and events.
—Pierre Pradervand

With each blessing you utter, your consciousness is raised and you help to raise the consciousness of those around you.
—Eileen Cady

Blessing rituals are practiced in a variety of rites and ceremonies across cultures, and in some form in almost every religion, though not all blessings are faith-based. Blessings offered outside of a religious context are often less formal. "Do I have your blessing?" is a way of asking for permission and "I give you my blessing" can mean simply that a person is granting a request or embracing a new idea or procedure. The phrase "God bless you" is said to have originated with Pope Gregory during the Black Plague as a small prayer to protect someone from death. At some point, it morphed into "Bless you" being the polite thing to say when someone sneezes. Large numbers of people in cultures around the world bless the food they are about to eat and the hands that prepared it, and many who reject organized religion still say grace.

The Mezuzah hung on doorposts in Jewish homes pronounces blessings on those who dwell within as well as all who enter the house; other religions have various ways of blessing a new house and/or the inhabitants of homes. There are also a multitude of rituals for blessing or cleansing one's home space conducted by any number of practitioners and guides from ceremonial artists to shamans to feng shui consultants.

Jesus exhorted his followers to not only to love our enemies, but to bless those that curse us. In today's society, people often seem more likely to curse than to bless one another. Stuck in traffic jams for instance, we may observe drivers shouting at each other with clenched fists or raised fingers, or hear curse words flying through the air. We witness sports fans hurling curses at a player, a referee, or an umpire. We may pass people on the street swearing into their cell phone because they disagree with the voice on the other end. What a difference it might make if we all chose to bless instead of curse when such impulses arise.

Though many have grown used to relying on religious leaders to bestow blessings, in fact, we all have the choice and the power to bless others if we have a pure intention to do so. Life presents us with myriad opportunities to practice the art of blessing. Blessings can take the form of supplication, praise, comfort, encouragement, or gratitude. A blessing can be vocalized, written, or silently sent as a meditative practice. We can direct a blessing to a specific individual such as a child, grandchild, or other loved one, to a parent, spouse, friend, neighbor, caregiver, teacher, or to a person who may have helped us in the past in some noteworthy way that we weren't aware of at the time. We need not wait for a designated once-a-year day to bless our land, our forests, fruit-bearing tress and vegetable gardens that nourish us, the earth on which we walk, and its natural resources which sustain us.

We might put our attention on groups of people with the aim of directing a simple blessing or affirmation to them: newborn infants, traumatized children, struggling teenagers, children separated from the families unfairly, politicians, musicians, journalists, janitors, doctors, nurses, firefighters, first responders, nursing-home residents, victims of sexual assault, the disabled, the disenfranchised among us, the homeless, those who struggling with addiction or mental illness, those who are angry, depressed, living with chronic pain, or nearing death, the recently bereaved, and so on.

A blessing can be written on a sign waved during peaceful protests, marches for justice, or as a way of expressing appreciation for the heroes in our collective lives. We can use blessings to express gratitude for gifts of all types. We can bless someone for a simple kindness: the stranger who offers a helping hand when we're grappling with a heavy bag, the doctor who takes the time to sit down and listen to our fears as we struggle to adjust to a life-threatening diagnosis, or the vet who comes out to the car to euthanize a beloved animal companion in our arms instead of inside the building. We can bless someone for his or her courage, leadership, generosity, or support. "May you be blessed for all you are doing to help the poor in our community," or "Bless you for coming to help feed the hungry today."

This practice, much like my gratitude practice, began spontaneously. I can't pinpoint the specific date, though I remember that I was in the middle of a mental gratitude list when it seemed to naturally morph into sending blessings to the individuals or groups I was expressing gratitude for. Like any mindfulness exercise done regularly, sending out blessings is an activity that yields greater benefits over time. I found that it is possible for us to bless those with whom we disagree, those we feel critical of, even those who may have mistreated or hurt us in the past. Although my birth mother died years before I developed this practice, I am able to bless her for giving birth to me, for letting me go instead of objecting or holding on when the judge made his pronouncement, and for her efforts to connect with me later in my life.

Major life challenges can turn out to be blessings in disguise. I am now able to look at unwished-for experiences such as my cancer diagnosis, which was daunting and scary at the time yet gave me exactly what I needed in to reset priorities, to let go of nonproductive habits and behaviors, to alter my diet and to eat more mindfully. Rather than wishing events in my past had been different, or pretending something never happened, I choose to look at the past as being what has brought me to my life in the present. From that perspective, whatever took place in the past can be perceived as a blessing. The Dalai Lama once said that if the Chinese government hadn't done what it did, he would never have had to evolve his heart to be larger than the pain they brought.

Historically, blessings are often reinforced by a gesture such as uplifted arms or laying-on of hands. When blessing someone directly, if the person is open to it, we can touch her or him in some way to deepen the connection and reinforce the words we are saying: a handshake, an open hand over the person's heart; an arm around shoulders, or any kind of appropriate touch that is safe and that the individual is willing to receive. More than once, I have been greeted with a "Bless you" when I merely stopped to smile or say hello, to an elderly resident sitting in an entryway or hallway of a care facility. Simple daily gestures such as a kiss on the cheek, a hand on the heart, or laying a hand for a moment on the head of a young child or while saying, "Have a good day," are essentially blessings, calling forth a wish for, and a vision of, safety and protection for a loved one.

The late Irish poet John O'Donohue writes about rediscovering our power to bless one another. In his book *To Bless the Space Between Us*, he defines a blessing as "a circle of light drawn around a person to protect, heal and strengthen," thus illuminating an individual or a situation in a new way. In his book, *The Gentle Art of Blessing*, Swiss author and sociologist Pierre Pradervand writes about blessing others as a way to "center ourselves in love," and says that when we bless others "without concern for their appearance, expression, race, class, sex, or any other label," it will expand our hearts. He points out that it is impossible to bless and judge at the same time and encourages us to hold fast to blessing as a sacred practice.

Forgiveness

Forgiving is giving up the hope that the past could have been different. True forgiveness is when you can say thank you for that experience.
—Oprah Winfrey

Forgiveness is a way to set down old pain. It liberates us from the wounds of our past.
—Frank Ostaseski

Most major religions include teachings on forgiveness. Innumerable books have been written by psychologists, researchers, and religious leaders, as well as everyday practitioners, that enumerate the psycho-social, emotional and spiritual benefits of forgiveness. The significance of forgiveness has been written about and extolled by many modern-day activists and teachers from Mother Theresa to Nelson Mandela to Pema

Chödrön. They have all communicated, in their own ways, the importance of developing and maintaining our ability to forgive, how essential forgiveness is in any healing process, and that forgiveness is a path to liberation and inner peace.

Renowned peace activist, Jack Kornfield, one of the key teachers to introduce Buddhist mindfulness practices to the west, has shared a number of remarkable stories concerning forgiveness. He tells one about sitting with the Dalai Lama and a group of Tibetan nuns who were imprisoned during their teenage years for praying out loud and refusing to give up their religion. They subsequently survived years of captivity and torture. In a meeting with a group of ex-prisoners from the United States, along with the now-released nuns, someone asked, "Were you ever afraid?" One of the women responded by saying that the thing they had feared most during their imprisonment was that they would succumb to hating their guards, that they would lose their compassion. The nuns reported that, while incarcerated, they had expressed their forgiveness for their captors through meditation practices. Another of the women in their group stated: "Just as we were incarcerated, our guards were not free. By doing their jobs and their duty, they were forced to be cruel."

It has been said that when we have experienced traumatic injury or abuse, we will never fully recover until we can forgive. My experience is that although forgiveness can manifest in a flash of new insight or awakening, it can also occur, little by little, as a process, over time. Either way, forgiveness is a life-changing practice.

When my birth mother appeared to me in such a surprising and intense way near the time of her death, and I kept repeating, "I forgive you," it was a reaction born out of compassion, without conscious effort. I felt some sort of relief, or release, after the encounter. When the incident subsequently came up after that, I was emotionally detached when repeating it, thinking, naively, that the complicated relationship with my birth mother had been sorted and settled. After completing an assignment in a graduate school class on Transforming Grief, which required accessing a deep wound in one's life and retelling the story as myth, I was certain that I had forgiven her on a deeper level.

Perusing the archival documents I received in the mail more than a decade later muddied the waters considerably, and threw me into an emotional tailspin. The new information exposed the depth of my mother's neglect and rejection, forcing me to face feelings that I had no idea were still buried in my subconscious. With some persistence and determination, for the first time in my life, I was able to access and express those buried feelings emotionally and physically. As cathartic as that proved to be, there was an even deeper release to come.

While contemplating the meaning of forgiveness more deeply, I came across a Thich Nhat Hanh interview with Oprah Winfrey, a version of which I had actually watched when it occurred in 2013, about a year and a half before Hanh suffered the stroke that limited his walking and speaking ability.

In responding to a question Winfrey asked him about suffering, the eighty-five-year-old peace activist responded: "The first step in the art of transforming suffering is to come home to our suffering and recognize it. . . and the second step is for us to embrace it." Those last few words were mind stopping. I hit the pause button and took a few deep breaths while letting the thought of that second step percolate.

Thich Nhat Hanh's countenance and distinctive way of speaking opened my heart as he introduced the idea that our bodies and our minds hold not only our own suffering, but also the unresolved suffering of our parents and of their parents, and so on, handed down from generation to generation, "because no one knew how to recognize, embrace, and heal it. It's not your fault, nor is it their fault."

This gentle sage then used an unusual term—"unskillfulness"—as something we all have in relating to others.

> The other person may not want to make us suffer or to hurt us. People can become victims of their own suffering. . . Without that understanding, forgiving is difficult. If you can understand the deep suffering in him or her, the situation becomes different. You can forgive more easily.

With great clarity and composure, he went on to say: "If we can heal our wounded child, we will not only liberate ourselves, but we will also help liberate whoever has hurt or abused us."

It has long been my experience that when we are ready, the teaching we need will appear in some form. An extraordinary thing occurred for me as I listened to this benevolent monk speaking with such certainty and compassion. His words simply landed. In that moment, I experienced an opening inside my being, a visceral feeling, as if some giant weight had been extracted. A sudden rush of energy filled me, along what I could only describe as euphoria. I wanted to move, to dance, to sing, to thank and to praise the Divine. It was as if I had been shackled and was suddenly set free. I rose from my chair and began spontaneously moving around the space in ways I had not moved in years.

I open to my birth mother's suffering. Of course she was in pain, of course she was wounded. She was suffering before she met my father, before I was born, her entire life. The choices she made grew out of the suffering of her mother and father, and perhaps from their parents as well. She was unable to heal the wounded child inside her. She was unskillful in the way she cared for me as a baby, and yet she was doing the best she could at the time. And it wasn't my fault. I was not to blame. I was never not enough. I was never unworthy of love. I forgive her. I forgive myself . . . there is nothing to forgive.

In that timeless moment, I let go of the ghosts of the past. Whatever shards of blame I was still carrying in regard to the woman who gave birth to me simply dropped away, dematerialized, vanished. I became cognizant of the fact that, in subtle ways, I had been wishing I could have had a different mother, a different beginning to my life. Yet if my life had unfolded differently, I wouldn't be the same person I am today. Perhaps I was given the parents who facilitated my entrance into this world, and the exact experiences I needed in order to evolve, to help me wake up.

The "story" about what occurred during my first year of life, and other parts of my childhood, is truly irrelevant. My thoughts about it are irrelevant. They don't have to keep taking up any space inside my brain, or my heart any longer, as they only serve to keep me from being fully present in my life, in the here and now.

A translated quote from the 13th century mystic and poet, Rumi, pierces my consciousness, "The wound is the place where the Light enters you." That perspective changes everything. Without the darkness, how would we find a path to the light? I feel as if I've been thrown through a portal into another dimension. Peace washes over me like a river.

"The Healing Time"

Finally on my way to yes
I bump into
all the places

where I said no
to my life
all the untended wounds
the red and purple scars

those hieroglyphs of pain
carved into my skin,
my bones,
those coded messages
that send me down
the wrong street

again and again
where I find them
the old wounds
the old misdirections
and I lift them
one by one

close to my heart
and I say holy
holy

—Pesha Joyce Gertler

With Gratitude to . . .

. . . my husband, Barry Barankin, for not only helping me become a better writer, but for seeing me, listening to me, accepting me, encouraging me, loving me, walking with me through countless challenges and changes, and for persistently supporting me in myriad ways for over forty years;

. . . Doug, for choosing me, loving me and helping me bring two amazing beings into this world, for remaining my friend after neither of us was able to sustain the vows we had made, for encouraging me to marry again, for co-parenting with us until your sudden, untimely death;

. . . the three remarkable individuals—Brianna, Michael and Meghan—whom I've been blessed to call my children in this lifetime, for pushing all my "buttons," calling out the best in me and being my most significant teachers. You (along with your life partners, Ken, Sally and Kelly) continue to inspire me as you reach new goals, parent children of your own, strive to make the world a better place, and gift me with your continuing love and adult friendship;

. . . Lawrence for forty years of mentorship, support, wise counsel, and for your unique voice and generosity in contributing to this book;

. . . Cecily for an ever-deepening friendship, your unflappable optimism, keen mental discernment, generosity of spirit, and always prescient insights;

. . . Stephan and Katya who know nearly everything there is to know about me and still love me, and for being exemplary first responders in any crisis;

. . . Joanne for a sustaining friendship and for being someone I can always count on to celebrate, commiserate, laugh or cry with me, or to simply listen;

. . . my "Moms Over Forty" Support Group—drawn together over thirty years ago by our decision to become mothers for the first time, or again, after the age of forty—for the continuity of our connection, for wisdom, fellowship, tears, and laughter shared, and for sisterhood as we continue to adjust to life's changes and challenges;

. . . Chavurah Alef, a distinctive group of Jewish, and honorary Jewish men and woman whose pot luck Shabbat gatherings, volunteer projects, Jewish Renewal holidays, bat mitzvah and other celebrations as our daughters have grown into adults, mourning our elders as they've left this earth, and countless other shared rituals, have enriched my life for over a quarter century;

. . . author/teachers who have shaped and shaken my thinking, heartened, and inspired me for decades: Pema Chödrön, Ram Das, Natalie Goldberg, Thich Nhat Hahn, Jack Kornfield, Stephen Levine, Frank Ostaseski, Helen Palmer, Eckhart Tolle, Jon Kabat-Zinn, and more recently, Roshi Joan Halifax, Gabor Maté, Zainab Salbi and Steve Taylor.

. . . the multitude of writers, poets, artists, musicians, bodyworkers, therapists, retreat leaders, students, and colleagues, as well as fellow seekers on the path who, together with my wonderfully diverse, talented, and caring extended family and friends, have provided me with motivation and inspiration over the years;

. . . Melissa Shields at the Kentucky Department for Libraries and Archives who persisted in searching for information that might shed light on my early history and mailed me what turned out to be illuminating documents;

. . . Goldie, Karen, Kathryn, Kelly Linda, Marla, Willow, and other friends across the globe for enthusiastic words of encouragement, proofreading, helpful ideas, and useful advice, technical and otherwise;

. . . my trustworthy trio of editors: Barry, who marked my chapter drafts as the grammarian and English teacher extraordinaire that he is; Cecily, who read innumerable drafts of my writing offering both practical and prudent suggestions in the most positive of ways; and Meg, the best young line editor I know, a professional writer and editor for nearly a decade before deciding to go to law school where she, naturally, became an executive editor of the Law Review;

. . . and to Matthew Félix without whose help this book might have had a much longer gestation period.

I bow to you all.

Suggested Reading

Chödrön, Pema, *Taking the Leap: Freeing Ourselves from Old Habits and Fears*, Boston, Massachusetts, Shambhala Publications, Inc., 2009.

Chödrön, Pema, *The Wisdom of No Escape: and the Path of Loving-Kindness*, Boston & London, Shambhala, 1991.

Gil, Eliana, PhD, *Outgrowing the Pain: A Book for and About Adults Abused as Children*, NY, Dell Publishing, 1983.

Hahn, Thich Nhat, *No Mud No Lotus: The Art of Transforming Suffering*, Berkeley, California, Parallax Press, 2014.

Hahn, Thich Nhat, *RECONCILIATION: Healing the Inner Child*, Berkeley, California, Parallax Press, 2010.

Harris, Nadine Burke, M.D., *The Deepest Well: Healing the Long-Term Effects of Childhood Adversity*, NY, NY Houghton Mifflin Harcourt, 2018.

Hooks, Emily J., *The Power of Forgiveness: A Guide to Healing and Wholeness*, Forgiveness Academy, US, 2017.

Kornfield, Jack, *A Path with Heart: A Guide Through the Perils and Promises of Spiritual Life*, NY, NY, A Bantam Book, Random House, Inc., 1993.

Levine, Peter A. with Ann Frederick, *Walking the Tiger: Healing Trauma*, Berkeley, California, North Atlantic Books, 1997.

Matousek, Mark, *Writing to Awaken: A Journey of Truth, Transformation & Self-Discovery*, Oakland, California, Reveal Press, 2017.

Miller, Alice, *The Truth Will Set You Free: Overcoming Emotional Blindness and Finding Your True Adult Self* (Andrew Jenkins, translator), NY, Basic Books, 2001.

Noyes, Lawrence, *The Enlightenment Intensive: The Power of Dyad Communication for Self-Realization*, United Kingdom, Zenways Press, 2018.

O'Donohue, John, *To Bless the Space Between Us: A Book of Blessings*, NY, Doubleday, 2008

Pradervand, Pierre, *The Gentle Art of Blessing: A Simple Practice that Will Transform You and Your World*, NY, NY, Atria Paperback, 2009.

Salzberg, Sharon, *Faith: Trusting Your Own Deepest Experience*, NY, Riverhead Books, 2002

Salbi, Zainab, *Freedom is an Inside job: Owning our Darkness and our Light Healing Ourselves and the World*, Boulder, Colorado, Sounds True, 2018.

Taylor, Steve, *Out of the Darkness: From Turmoil to Transformation*, Carlsbad, California, Hay House, Inc., 2011.

Tolle, Eckhart, *The Power of Now: A Guide to Spiritual Enlightenment*, Novato, California, New World Library, 2004.

About the Author

Dawn spent the first few years of her life in Kentucky, grew up in Kansas, and graduated from colleges in Nebraska and Texas before landing in California in 1968. Her journey took her from minister's wife and mother to graduate school to professional actress to massage practitioner to meditation teacher and residential retreat leader. Completing a two-year certification course in "Awakening to Life and Death" in 1990 inspired Dawn to create the COMPASSIONATE TOUCH for Those in Later Life Stages™ program (www.fromtheheart-hands.com). Now semi-retired, Dawn lives with her husband in the California Bay Area where she continues to write, deepen her meditative practices, and spend time, as often as possible, with her three adult children, four grandchildren, and three grand-dogs.

Made in the USA
Columbia, SC
08 September 2021